"With Second Wind for the Second Half, *Patrick Morley again proves that he is one of the most dear and relevant voices speaking to Christian men and men's issues of our day. Like a good coach at 'half-time,' Morley helps men evaluate their past mistakes and provides the kind of practical insights, encouragement, and inspiration that will help them 'run to win' the rest of the way—and to reach their full potential in Christ."*

BILL MCCARTNEY

FOUNDER AND CEO, PROMISE KEEPERS

"Morley's analogy of the 'midlife lake' is worth the price of the book. He asks the right questions and rightly predicts that your 'second half' can be the most significant part of your life."

BOB BUFORD

AUTHOR, *HALFTIME*

"Patrick Morley doesn't just write a book, he inscribes truth on the tablets of the heart and puts an imprint on the pages of the mind."

EDWIN LOUIS COLE

FOUNDER AND PRESIDENT, CHRISTIAN MEN'S NETWORK

"Patrick Morley takes the need for wisdom seriously and dispenses it generously. He is convinced that the midlife era can be a starting line, not an end point. There is great discernment and encouragement in this book."

JOHN ORTBERG

AUTHOR, *THE LIFE YOU'VE ALWAYS WANTED* AND *LOVE BEYOND REASON*

Resources by Patrick Morley

Devotions for Couples
The Man in the Mirror
The Rest of Your Life
Second Wind for the Second Half
Second Wind for the Second Half audio
The Seven Seasons of a Man's Life
Walking with Christ in the Details of Life
What Husbands Wish Their Wives Knew About Men
What Husbands Wish Their Wives Knew About Men audio

Second Wind for the
SECOND HALF

TWENTY IDEAS TO HELP YOU

REINVENT YOURSELF

FOR THE REST OF THE JOURNEY

PATRICK MORLEY
author of THE MAN IN THE MIRROR

ZondervanPublishingHouse
Grand Rapids, Michigan

A Division of HarperCollinsPublishers

Second Wind for the Second Half
Copyright © 1999 by Patrick M. Morley

Requests for information should be addressed to:

ZondervanPublishingHouse
Grand Rapids, Michigan 49530

Library of Congress Cataloging-in-Publication Data

Morley, Patrick M.
    Second wind for the second half : twenty ideas to help you reinvent yourself for the rest of
the journey / Patrick M. Morley.
        p.   cm.
    ISBN 0-310-22132-3 (alk. paper)
    1. Middle-aged persons—Religious life.   I. Title.
    BV4579.5 M68 1998
    248.8'4—ddc21   98-37484
                                                  CIP

This edition printed on acid-free paper and meets the American National Standards Institute
Z39.48 standard.

All Scripture quotations, unless otherwise indicated, are taken from the *Holy Bible: New
International Version*®. NIV®. Copyright © 1973, 1978, 1984 by International Bible Society. Used
by permission of Zondervan Publishing House. All rights reserved.

Scripture quotations marked THE MESSAGE are from *The Message*. Copyright © 1993, 1994, 1995.
Used by permission of NavPress Publishing Group.

Published in association with Wolgemuth and Associates, Inc., 330 Franklin Road #135A-106,
Brentwood, TN 37027

Interior design by Sherri L. Hoffman

Printed in the United States of America

99 00 01 02 03 04 05 /❖ DC/ 10 9 8 7 6 5 4 3 2 1

To my dad, Bob Morley.
Among all the men I have known,
you are the most honorable.
How I loved growing up at your feet.
You have been my inspiration.
The way you lived your second half
has shown me the path that I, too, must travel.
I want to be like you, Dad.
I want to make you proud.

Contents

INTRODUCTION

ONE DAY AT THE AGE OF forty-eight, I was standing in our kitchen, ironing a dress shirt. As I worked the iron back and forth across the cotton, my thoughts began to drift. I saw myself standing in that exact same spot doing the exact same thing ten years later at the age of fifty-eight.

Frankly, I was startled. I wondered, *What will have changed ten years from now?* The answer seemed to be "nothing," unless I began to put some things in motion now. That's what this book is all about—putting some things in motion so that you will be pleased with who you become over the next ten years.

My fascination with the midlife experience began in 1974. As a young, aspiring twenty-five-year-old real estate broker, I sold a building for a man mired down in problems at the midpoint of his life.

Donald (as with all names in this book, this one has been changed) had been the shooting star, the proverbial golden boy, of the Orlando real estate market. His company got caught in an upward spiral of ever-increasing development successes. When a severe recession hit in the early 1970s, the overhead "nut" and debt payments brought his whole leveraged empire tumbling down on him.

Actually, I met Donald after all the employees had left, after he had left his wife, and the dust was starting to settle. He was darkly depressed, living alone in his office. And it was a real pigsty. Trash, dirty clothes, file folders, microwave dinner tins, and Chinese take-out boxes were strewn and piled everywhere. In addition, he had moved all his remaining earthly possessions into this one room in the building he wanted to sell—one of his few remaining assets. He wanted to sell, it turned out, so that he could run away on his sailboat. I was there because I had a buyer for the building.

I must tell you, however, that there was something about this man that struck a deep chord within me. Even though Donald was despondent, mopey, and hard to talk to, he still possessed a shadow of that charisma that had led to such meteoric success. I couldn't help but like him.

As I scanned his hovel of an office I could scarcely take it in. It shocked my sensibilities; it was chaos. Yet there amid the filth and scattered business papers, my eyes fell on the only semblance of order, symmetry, and beauty in the entire place. Standing elegantly on a credenza was a single, framed photograph of a small girl standing on the back of a sailboat.

As I studied the picture for a moment I noticed that Donald had made this photograph (consciously or not, I do not know) the focal point of his entire office and, because this office at that point was his entire life, the focal point of his existence.

"Who is that?" I asked.

At that, as if someone had opened a vacuum-packed can, fresh air rushed into the room. The heavy mood of the moment was immediately replaced by a light airiness, and he said with great pride and affection, "That's my daughter, Jennifer." Also, etched across the stern of the boat was the name *Jennifer*.

I was overwhelmed at how quickly the simple thought of his daughter had lifted the thick, gloomy clouds suspended in the air all about him. It was clear that Jennifer was the anchor of his soul, the slender thread tied to his spirit that kept him from drifting off into complete despair. The mere mention of her name gave him a second wind.

I was so deeply moved by the intensity of his love for her and the power that the mere mention of her name had to restore a sense of hope to his soul, that I vowed to myself if Patsy and I ever had a daughter her name would be Jennifer.

We did have a daughter. And her name is Jennifer.

By God's grace, very few of us will ever sink as deeply as Donald did into an all-out, old-fashioned midlife crisis. In fact, one of my purposes for writing this book is to show you how to avoid such a crisis. Yet virtually all of us will at some point be disappointed when life returns less than we expected.

If you are reading this book you are probably going through a midlife experience right now. Maybe you're just coming out of one, or suspect you're headed into one. Or perhaps your spouse is struggling.

The question is, when you do go through your midlife slump—whether a minor "funk" or a great ordeal—what will be the anchor for your soul? What will give you a semblance of order, symmetry, and beauty? What or who will be the focal point of your life? How will you replace the heavy moods? What will give you pride and love? What are the threads or ropes that will keep you from drifting away? How will you restore a sense of hope in your soul? Where will your "second wind" come from? These are the questions I hope to help you answer in this book as you reinvent yourself for the second half of the journey.

Some books seek to help those in crisis. By contrast, this book is written for the majority of us who, though not desperate enough for professional help, could use a hand to sort out midlife's sometimes bewildering sense of sadness and loss. I suggest using it for small group study. You may be surprised at how many others are facing the same issues you are.

The purpose of this book is to raise the issues common to all of us at midlife, to offer practical ideas to make peace with the changes that occur, and to show you how to reinvent yourself to experience a deeper, lasting sense of significance and joy during the second half of the journey.

I hope you will not simply read this book, but experience it. Let it be a time to take stock, a time to find humor, a time to adjust to the impossible changes taking place, a time to accept disappointment, a time to adjust your expectations and, most of all, a time to rediscover the joy of your humanity and your God.

My prayer and belief for you is that your second half will read like Job's: "The Lord blessed Job in the second half of his life even more than in the beginning" (Job 42:12 *New Living Translation*).

By the way, Donald eventually did come out of his difficult season and is doing well.

PART ONE

Midpoint

O N E

The New Meaning of Midlife—Not a Monolithic Experience

You cannot discover new lands unless you
leave shore for a very long time.
ANDRE GIDE

THE BEAUTIFUL, MYSTERIOUS ST. JOHNS RIVER meanders through central Florida not far from where we live. Near the headwaters the river runs swift, but the waters slow as the river deepens and the journey lengthens.

Halfway to its final destination, the river opens into a huge lake. Without its two banks, the river has no direction. The waters spread out and barely move. Each droplet of water entering the mouth of this lake travels a different course. But this is not the Dead Sea, so eventually two riverbanks gather the waters, and the river once again runs steady.

Midlife is like a lake. Early in our lives we run swift like a river, but shallow. As we put years behind us, though, we deepen. Then one day, we enter the opened jaws of midlife. Where once we felt direction and velocity, suddenly we find ourselves swirling about, sometimes aimlessly, or so it seems. Each of us, like individual droplets of water, will take a different path through this part of the journey. For some of us it will only be a slowdown. Others will feel forgotten and abandoned by the father of the river. Some, unable to see where the waters converge and once again grow strong, will despair.

Time, however, stops for no one and nothing. Eventually all the little droplets of water, however depressed they may be, find themselves regaining speed as the riverbanks once again gather the waters, point them forward, and give them purpose.

RESTRUCTURING AND CELEBRATION

Midlife is not a monolithic experience. Each of us will experience midlife in our own way. We cannot project at what age it will begin, how long it will last, or the intensity with which it will hit us. Each of us will drift through a different part of the lake. For some it will be a mere "slump"; for others a "funk"; for still others an all-out crisis. And, while midlife has no single cause, its issues are predictable. All must pass through this lake.

In the early 1990s the real estate industry was stunned when Olympia and York, the world's largest developer, declared bankruptcy. One analyst summed it up when he said, "Nobody is bigger than the market."

As there is a "restructuring" cycle in business, so there is a restructuring cycle in our private lives. This "reorganization" takes place sometime during our thirties, forties, or fifties and can span several years, even a decade. We call it midlife, though many of us would deny its existence and postpone its decisions. But nobody is bigger than the midlife experience. Nobody.

We each come to a moment when we must admit, even if only to ourselves, that things are changing. Some of us will embrace the changes, others will deny them as long as possible.

Though no one escapes the midlife experience, neither is it the end of the world. In fact, as we will see, midlife can become a rich, promising season of reinventing ourselves for the rest of the journey.

Before we can reinvent ourselves, though, we must first humbly admit we have reached the middle years. My wife, Patsy, and I became middle-aged on the same day. Here's how it happened.

One evening I was washing my face to get ready for bed, and I started laughing. Patsy, who was reading in bed, called out, "What's so funny?"

At that, I walked from the bathroom to the bedroom so she could see. As I had lathered up my face, I had forgotten to take off my glasses, and the lenses were coated with a thin film of soap punctuated with bubbles.

Patsy chuckled and said (this is a true story), "That's nothing! This morning I was trying to balance our checkbook, but I couldn't get the calculator to work. Finally, I looked down and realized I had been punching numbers into the portable telephone."

After we regained some composure we had to admit that, like the sixty thousand slaves who passed through Senegal's infamous "door of no return," we had passed through a "time portal" through which we could never return.

In this book I would like us to learn how to celebrate midlife. It can and should be an encouraging, growing time. It's a time to clean out closets. It's a time to unpack baggage we accumulated along the journey. It's a time to toss some things into the emotional dumpster.

Whether you have a mild case of "midlife slump" or find yourself in an all-out crisis, you're normal. And while we do need to deal with the issues raised by thirty-five, forty, fifty, or more years of neglect and imbalance, the real task of midlife—and our task together in this book—is to reinvent ourselves for the rest of the journey.

CHANGES IN THE LIFE CYCLE

The fundamental nature of the midlife experience is changing. According to researcher and writer Gail Sheehy, a revolution is taking place in the life cycle. She points out that when our parents turned fifty they thought of themselves as old. Not us, though. "Middle age has already been pushed far into the fifties—if it is acknowledged at all today. The territory of the fifties, sixties, and beyond is changing so radically that it now opens up whole new passages leading to stages of life that are nothing like what our parents or grandparents experienced. Fifty is now what forty used to be."[1]

The midlife experience can begin as early as the thirties or may stretch well into the fifties. Yet, the idea I would like to get across is that midlife is not so much an age as an experience.

Today we enjoy two phases of the life cycle our forefathers at the turn of the century did not experience: adolescence and midlife. Instead, our forebears began working from the earliest ages (typically on a farm) and died before they were old enough to wonder, "How will I spend the rest of my life?"

CHANGES IN LIFE EXPECTANCY: THE NEXT THIRTY YEARS

One morning, when I was forty-seven, I asked the 175 men at the Bible study I teach each Friday morning to stand. Next I asked all the men over fifty-seven to sit down, then said, "Today in Russia the life expectancy of a man is fifty-seven. For those of you sitting down right now, if you lived in Russia today—you're dead!"

Finally, I said, "In the Unites States during the year 1900 the average male life expectancy was forty-seven. If you're over forty-seven, you're dead. Sit down." By then roughly forty percent of the men had taken their seats. As I stood before them I pondered that if I, at the age of forty-seven, had lived in 1900, this would be the year I was expected to die.

It is by the grace of God through science, medical research, and technology that a litany of life-extending breakthroughs have lengthened life expectancy into the midseventies. Remarkable advances with sanitation, pesticides, fluoride, chlorine, medicine, diet, and hygiene have virtually doubled the quantity and quality of our productive adult lives.

Since 1900 the average life span has increased by nearly thirty years.[2] So the whole concept of "midlife" is a relatively new idea. And it is a blessing. Through increased prosperity and medical advances these additional thirty years (or more) will be the most productive, authentic years of your life. They will be decades of substance and stability.

At the turn of century what we now call midlife was the end of life. In 1950 it was the door to old age. The stereotype we must overcome is that the next step after reaching midlife is "getting old." The new "attitude" is that midlife symbolizes the gateway to a second adulthood—the second phase of *productive* adulthood.

When one of my best friends of twenty-five years turned fifty, we attended his surprise birthday party. He said he woke up a little down that morning, so he took the morning off to get a haircut and have some shoes repaired. Then his friends completely surprised him with a special luncheon. He was truly touched. Later he lamented that five-sevenths of his life was now over.

Actually, I think a better way to think of turning fifty is to say that the first half of your productive adult life is over. In other words, the first half of productive adult life is roughly twenty-five to fifty and the second half is from fifty to seventy-five. When thought of this way, it puts an entirely different spin on fifty.

Midlife promises not to be a door to a dungeon but a window that opens onto a whole new life of renewal and celebration. Don't think of your "life" expectancy in the single category of "time." In addition, you have a "productive" expectancy, a "health" expectancy, a "family life" expectancy, and a "financial" expectancy. Can you think of other expectancies?

The real issue is not that we reach "the middle," but how do we spend (or invest) the extra thirty years that medicine and technology, by God's grace, have bequeathed us?

We must, however, deal with two problems to get there. We need a new picture of the future, and we must go through a transition.

A New Picture of the Future

First, we need a new understanding of the future. We are the first generation that has peered down the corridor of time and been able to envision a healthy, vibrant seventy-five-year-old picture. A healthy fifty-year-old woman today can expect to live until she is eighty-one; a healthy fifty-year-old man until he is seventy-six.[3]

NBA Hall of Fame coach Chuck Daly became the head coach of the Orlando Magic at sixty-seven. Quality expert Phil Crosby bought back his company at seventy. John Glenn boarded the space shuttle at seventy-seven. Billy Graham held crusades at eighty. The average age of a Supreme Court Justice at the turn of the century is sixty-six, (four of them are over sixty-five, and Justice Blackmun retired at eighty-five). Two of my closest friends and leaders in our organization are still active in the business world, one at seventy-two and the other at seventy-eight. Speaker and motivator Paul Meyer climbed the tallest mountain in America at seventy.

While these examples from our parents' generation somewhat defy the norm, they represent "early models" of what will define the norm for our generation. In other words, when you turn seventy the Chuck Daly/Phil Crosby experiences will be normative, not exceptional. Baby boomers will redefine what it means to be sixty-five, seventy, and seventy-five. In fact, they (we) will demand useful, productive lives.

This means we must develop a whole new pattern for thinking about these thirty years. They are no longer "golden" in the sense of laid back, retiring times. Instead, they look "platinum." They hold promise for vitality, contribution, and love. For most of us these thirty years will be larger, more creative, more freedom filled, and more exciting. Everyone knows aged wine is better than new.

Personally, I doubt that many of us from our generation will retire to little condominium pods where we stand waist deep in the swimming pool, wear straw hats by day, and play bingo in the recreation hall by night. Instead, we will reinvent new avenues of enterprise and loving service to humankind. Where do you visualize yourself at seventy-five?

Changes in the Meaning of Midlife: The Next One to Ten Years

Second, somewhere near the middle of our adult productive lives all of us will go through a transition. William Bridges called it "the neutral zone."[4] Bob Buford has coined the hopeful term "halftime."[5] Gail Sheehy calls it a "passage." I have used the analogy of a river slowing as it opens into a lake, before once again regaining speed between two defining banks.

William Bridges describes a transition like midlife as an ending of a phase, followed by a neutral zone, and then a new beginning. To enter the highly productive, healthy years ahead we must first pass through this "neutral zone"—the "lake"—between the first and second phases of our productive adult lives.

Some of us will find ourselves pouring into this lake as early or late, but most of us will flow into midlife between thirty-five and fifty-five. Some of us may only spend one year in the lake; others as much as a decade. Some may find themselves in the lake in their thirties or forties, then in another lake downstream again in their fifties.

During the middle years we each come to episodes of self-assessment when we wonder if we have taken the right path. We ask, "Who have I become? How did I get here? Is this who I really am and want to be? How can I reinvent myself so the rest of my journey really matters?" It is a time of introspection and self-examination.

We will find ourselves asking "real" questions. Either we have achieved our goals and are wondering, *So what? Where do I go from here?* Or we failed and are wondering, *Why me? What happens now?*

MAKING MIDLIFE CHANGES

Because of what happened to Donald, the man I mentioned in the introduction, throughout my thirties and forties I braced myself for a "midlife crisis." I worried that I would desert my senses, make horrible mistakes, embarrass my family, and become a fool. That never happened. Instead, at around thirty-seven, as my tired ship pulled unnoticed into the lake, I became bored. I yearned for a "new thing." I craved a more "spiritual" life. But I didn't know what to do.

Then a "northeaster" swept across the lake, and I found myself leaping into the lifeboat. For the next nine years I bobbed like a cork on sometimes calm, sometimes stormy waters. My midlife "lake" experience was a mini-series of twenty or so reassessments, adjustments, and reorganizations. I thank God for those nine years. I became a stronger, more intentional person from those years of fighting the elements in my lonely little lifeboat. While the boat I built during the first half sank, God gave me a life raft that would not sink.

I made three major changes while navigating the midlife lake. First, I changed careers after nineteen years. For six years I sensed a new "calling" and direction. Finally, while bobbing about in the storm, I did something about it. I thank God for the storm. The increase in meaning and purpose more than makes up for the short-term pain. It was, in hindsight, a cheap price to pay.

Second, I changed the core value of my life. My highest human value had always been "competence." I have always loved to observe anything done well. My obsession with excellence, though, left a vacuum in my soul for "beauty." Now I look for the beauty in all of God's creation, whether people, places, or ideas. Also, after eighteen years in the same house, we moved to a home that captures the grace of "old" architectural ideas reminiscent of America's colonial period.

Third, I became a recovering materialist. I stopped pursuing money as a coequal goal with God. I reorganized my schedule to permit more time alone with God each day. These three changes, for me, were huge. Over a nine-year period, without my going off the deep end, God helped me reinvent myself for the second half of my journey. What major changes have you made, or thought of making?

TRIGGERS

The next two decades will be phenomenally exciting as seventy-five million baby boomers (born 1946–1964), racing through the crowded canals of our shrink-wrapped culture, find themselves drifting in the lake. In the next twenty years millions of people will reorganize and reinvent themselves for the second half of their productive adult lives.

In early 1997 David Letterman turned fifty. He said, "This is the first birthday that's gotten my attention since I turned twenty-one when that was the legal drinking age. It dawned on me that there's no U-turn on this road." For Letterman, the river apparently dumped him into the lake at fifty.

For some, the trip wire for this experience is an event—a birthday, achieving a life goal, a silent house, the birth of a grandchild, a look in the mirror. For others, it's more like a silent alarm triggered by a barely visible accumulation of imperceptible changes that cannot be put into words. Still others pass into the lake through a calamity like the loss of a job or business, a brush with death, or the loss of a parent. Yet others feel a growing sadness and loss of spunk—one person described it as hitting a "wall of molasses."

WHAT ABOUT "A CRISIS AT THE MIDDLE OF LIFE"?

Twenty-five years ago the idea of "a midlife crisis at forty" was valuable because culture was still fairly homogeneous. In today's "choice" culture the mouth of the lake can easily open up ten years earlier or shift fifteen years further downstream. So the feeling that it's time to "reinvent" can come at a variety of ages.

THE WORD "MIDLIFE" AND A POSITIVE APPROACH

The use of the word "midlife" is the true conundrum for this book, a Gordian knot. It carries a lot of baggage.

The word "midlife" sends a negative message that you're getting older in a culture where older often means "no longer useful." Yet, because of prior usage, no other word gives quite the same "shorthand" meaning about the time period we are talking about. Still, the term confuses people and doesn't really express what we are talking about—a season of reinventing yourself for the second half of the journey.

What's the answer? We cannot jettison the "midlife" word itself because it is so integral to the common body of thought on this subject. But we can use many other words to enrich and nuance to our meaning. We need to create a new positive language that redefines the "conversation" about the midlife experience. So from the very start, we will weave into every part of every chapter that this book is about reinventing yourself for the rest of the journey, giving visible, positive brush strokes from cover to cover.

WHY WE NEED TO REINVENT AT ALL

Today most people will have either reached their life goals, decided those goals cannot be met, or be living through the death of their dream. The point is, they are at a "point." Because in today's world they now have twenty, thirty, or more years of productive life remaining, they possess the unique opportunity to reinvent themselves for the rest of the journey.

The old paradigm was "over the hill." So to be at the midpoint was to be "on" the hill. The only prospect was to go downhill. I think today's midpoint is more like standing on a plateau than lying draped over the top of a hill, looking down. Still, it took a lot of huffing and puffing to climb up to that plateau. We may even be a little slumped over trying to catch a breath and decide where to go from here. What we need now is to gather second wind for the second half of the climb.

FOCUS QUESTIONS

1. Are you in the midlife lake? If so, how long has it been, and do you see any end in sight?
2. Which description would best characterize your midlife experience, and why:

   • Business as usual?
   • A slight slowdown?
   • A slump?

- A funk?
- An all-out crisis?

3. Which of these scenarios best describes you, and why?

- I achieved my goals and wonder, *So what? Where do I go from here?*
- I didn't get what I wanted and wonder, *Why me? What happens now?*
- I am content.

4. Ask yourself these questions of self-assessment:

- Who have I become?
- How did I get here?
- Have I become who I wanted to be?

5. What have been your preconceived notions about the second half of life? (Think in terms of life expectancy, concept of retirement, what you will give yourself to.) How has your thinking been challenged in this chapter?

6. What are the areas of your life where you need to find a second wind? What major changes have you made or thought of making?

7. Where do you visualize yourself living and what do you visualize yourself doing at fifty-five? sixty-five? seventy-five?

T W O

A Wounded Dream—A Life That's Not Turning Out Like You Planned

"For I know the plans I have for you," declares the LORD,
*"plans to prosper you and not to harm you, plans to give you
hope and a future."*

JEREMIAH 29:11

FOR MANY YEARS NOW I HAVE listened closely to how men describe themselves at the halfway mark of their productive adult lives. The following story, synthesized from many different conversations, captures what I believe people in midlife are feeling inside these days.

As the Decades Go By

I can hardly believe how quietly yesterday came and went, almost completely unnoticed. It was my fiftieth birthday—a cruel reminder of how inconsequential my life has become. My wife bought a card, and one of my three children called, but that was it. I have some buddies I play golf with, but they never seem to be interested in anything except the next club tournament.

When I was in my forties I had an operation for a bad back. The office sent some flowers, but no one ever came to visit. I was out of work for two months, and my boss seemed more irritated than sympathetic about it. Before the operation I consumed aspirin like popcorn. I'm still stiff most every day.

In my thirties the kids demanded most of Judy's time, and she adored each one of them. I loved to toss the kids in the air. They would always laugh and giggle. They never had any doubt I would catch them. Now Judy works as an interior designer. The kids are gone and we must not have much in common, because she has really poured herself into her work.

In my twenties I was an idealist. I really thought I could change the world—shape it to my way of thinking. My positive attitude pleased my bosses, and they constantly increased my responsibilities. I love to have responsibility. But I found out quick that when I blundered, the credits I had accumulated didn't matter that much. When I was twenty-nine they passed me over for promotion and picked another man instead. That kind of shook my confidence, but I learned to conceal my disappointment. Now I don't really have any great ambitions. I would rather retreat and watch cable sports.

During my teen years my dad and I couldn't communicate. I have come to believe he loved me, but I don't think a seventeen-year-old is capable of discerning that on his own—he needs to hear it and feel it. So I wasn't that good at expressing love to my kids, either. And now it looks to be shaping up that I will reap from them what I sowed.

Until I was nine years old life was pure joy for me. I remember a few incidents with other kids hurting my feelings, but basically my world was filled with tranquillity. I never thought life had a dark side until our favorite cocker spaniel was hit by a car. She died slowly. I watched. I never quite felt carefree again after that experience. Now, of course, I have experienced hundreds of disappointments with life. And yet, I've often wondered if heaven will be like those carefree childhood memories.

THE PROBLEM

We all know early in life we will not become the president of the United States, but not until midlife does it sink in that we may not become any kind of president at all.

Midlife is the season of the disappointed dreamer. By the middle years we have each been stung by of a series of major disappointments that can lead to a deep sense of loss and bewilderment.

In many ways, midlife is that season when we wrestle with the question of "giving up or going on." Actually, we all make it through, but at the time the experience can seem as useless as it does painful.

Some of us who achieved our dream must now try to remember why we thought it was so important—not to mention if it was worth the price.

Others must come to grips with the fact that their oyster doesn't have a pearl. "I had a dream once. It died when nobody cared." It's okay to holler.

Twenty or more years of adult striving has led to a bottleneck. Life can develop a "sameness." We wonder, *Isn't there a higher calling than to be a _____ all my life? There must be more.*

THE MIDLIFE "FUNK"

A friend and I were talking about the midlife "funk." He said, "You know, my life is great in every way. Yet I find that I am struggling." Why do we end up in a funk somewhere in the middle of our adult lives, often at the very moment things are going well?

My friend said, "The hardest thing I'm dealing with at forty-six is getting comfortable being me." Why is this still a problem for us when we have already lived half our lives? It's because at our personal midpoint we finally realize that we are not going to be Billy Graham or Steven Jobs or Trammel Crow or whoever our hero is. Midlife is the place when we come to say, "I'm not ever going to be _____. I've got to learn how to be happy being me."

There is good news. Yes, at midlife some dreams do die; yet the joy of a new and better journey beckons to be discovered.

Why do dreams die, what does that death mean, and how can you go about finding a new dream?

WHY DO DREAMS DIE?

Some dreams were never meant to be. The only dreams that will come true are the dreams that are in God's will. Regrettably, when we are young we often develop our dreams out of our own imagination, creativity, and ambition without submitting them humbly before God for his approval, correction, and redirection.

Unfortunately, many of us have spent the first half of our productive adult lives pursuing our own purposes. The reason we have failed in reaching our dream is precisely that—it was *our* dream. Or, if by bulldog determination you were able to muscle your dream into reality, that's why you now wonder, *Why did I pay such a steep price for this? Why does success leave me thinking, "So what?" Why do I feel so empty and unfulfilled?*

Often, God has a different direction altogether for our lives, but sometimes it takes a couple of decades for our "other" ambition to run its course. Then, in the desolation of midlife we finally become quiet enough to hear "the still small voice" of God. He was always calling out to us, of course, but we created so much noise with our own plans that we drowned out his plans. Now we have become quiet—contrite really—and we are able to hear.

And what do we hear? "I wanted to give that dream to someone else. I have an even better dream for you, one that fits the way you have been wired." Or, "While that dream would have been exciting for you, the price you would have had to pay in other areas of your life would have been too high. I didn't allow that dream for your own good."

Why Your Dream Has Not Turned Out Like You Planned

Most of my dreams have not turned out like I planned, and I'll bet yours haven't, either. I used to think that God gave each of us a "fuzzy" dream like a half-developed Polaroid picture. Then, as we would keep moving toward it, the picture would become more clear.

Lately, however, I see that my dreams have developed differently. Instead, I now see that God gives us a dream that we start moving toward. But halfway there, the picture gets torn up, and we receive a new, slightly different dream. Yet, we could not pursue the new dream if we had not already come halfway toward the now discarded dream. There was something gained while pursuing the discarded dream that prepared us to go after the new dream.

As we change direction and move toward the new dream for a season, the cycle repeats. Again, the picture gets torn up, another new dream comes into focus, and God leads us off on a new angle. God, it seems, doesn't lead us by a single, increasingly clear vision. Rather, he leads by a series of smaller dreams that he successively fashions in our minds.

After college I knew I wanted to be in commercial real estate, but that was about all I could see. As it turned out, a man took me under his wing and mentored me for a year in the art of forming partnerships to buy land. A dream took shape, and I moved in that direction. After sixteen land deals I sensed the market changing, and my dream shifted to acquiring existing income-producing buildings. Actually, the market was soft at the time and the buildings were empty, so we formed partnerships to purchase empty buildings, then fixed them up and leased them out.

After we put together partnerships on sixteen existing buildings, the leasing market tightened up, and it was hard to find good deals. So the dream shifted again and we started developing buildings from the ground up.

Here's the point: I had no idea how many "different" paths I would take. I had no idea I would ever become a developer. My dream started in one direction, changed when the market shifted, then changed again. The dream came true, but in the beginning I didn't have a clue about what "success" would look like. The dream came true, but not like I planned. I'll bet you've experienced the same process. Our dreams change as we interact with opportunities, get blocked, and adjust to a changing environment. Why does it happen that way?

The apostle Paul had a dream. After a highly successful mission trip throughout Asia, he wanted to return to strengthen the work he had begun.

Here's what happened. On his second trip Paul wanted to take Barnabas who was with him on the first trip. But it didn't work out, and he ended up taking a man named Silas instead.

He wanted to go into Asia, but that didn't work out either. He was blocked from going in.

Next he tried to enter a region called Bithynia (a part of present-day Turkey), but he was unable to go there either.

Finally, the doors opened up for him to go to the altogether different region of Macedonia (present-day Greece), a place it had never occurred to him to visit.

The result of all these dream changes was that two traveling teams were sent out instead of one (Barnabas went in a different direction with another man), Europe received the gospel, many new churches were started that would not have otherwise begun, and many new converts came to faith.

Essentially, nothing Paul wanted or expected turned out the way he had planned. Yet everything turned out exactly the way God wanted. It didn't turn out like Paul dreamed; it turned out better. The apostle Paul had a significant impact on the world, perhaps second only to Jesus. It should be of great comfort to us that things rarely turned out like he planned.

And so here is my conclusion. See if this doesn't ring true to you: Because God is good, our lives will not turn out like we plan. They will turn out better.

"But wait just a minute!" you say. "For sure, my life hasn't turned out like I planned, but it's hardly better! I didn't get the mate I wanted. I didn't get the job I hoped for. I was passed over for the promotion that was the desire of my heart. We don't live in the city we wanted. My children are unappreciative. I've lost money. I've hurt people. I haven't come anywhere close to achieving my potential. And you say it's better? I don't think so!"

Who's to say? You don't know the "other option" of what may have happened in your life. Also, God is good, and God will use everything that has happened, good and bad, as the ingredients of a joyful journey when you make your peace with him and submit to the purpose of his will.

"But God has stopped me from doing the very thing I most wanted to do," you say. Consider this. When God takes away a dream, in due time he replaces it with a new, better thing he wants you to do. It may be a "larger" calling, or it may be "smaller" but more suited to your capabilities and, therefore, more joyful. It may, from a worldly perspective, be a smaller calling, but it will be better. All of your life will eventually turn out exactly like God planned. The only question is, will you accept and embrace his plan like a compliant child, or will you kick and fuss like a rebellious child? In either case, eventually, the Father will have his own way with each of us.

So, how does this relate to your wounded or dying dream? Let it die. God has a new, better dream for you waiting to be uncovered.

YOUR LIFE HAS MATTERED AND WILL CONTINUE TO MATTER

No movie touches the heart at Christmas more than the favorite Jimmy Stewart movie of all time, *It's a Wonderful Life*.

George Bailey, a despondent banker in the small town of Bedford Falls, describes himself as a failure. He takes us on a dark journey through his disappointed dreams, at the end of which he contemplates suicide on Christmas Eve.

Movie expert Jeanine Basinger said, "George Bailey is the guy who wanted more from life; he wanted to get out of town, do exciting things. Instead, he has what a lot of us have at holidays: a job, a family, a house that's falling apart."

Columnist Ellen Goodman of the Washington Post Writers Group believes this movie resonates more with our times than when originally released fifty years ago, because it is a movie about midlife.[1]

By anybody's actuarial table, the 1990s was the decade that a whole generation started hitting midlife. On arrival at midlife, everyone, to some extent, looks around and sees limits. That's why we identify with George Bailey. The American Dream that started out as Horatio Alger has come to look more like the life of George Bailey.[2]

Happily for George, in the movie, Clarence the angel takes him on a tour of what Bedford Falls would be without George Bailey. As Clarence says, a missing person "leaves an awful hole." It takes an angel to convince George that his life has mattered. Clarence shows George that his life does have meaning. It's a happy ending.

Your life has mattered too. If you engaged in an honorable vocation, loved God, invested in friends, served in a local congregation, offered yourself in community service, possibly married and brought children into the world, raised a family, and were a diligent provider, you have fulfilled God's purposes for your life to this point. Yes, the flame may have died down, but don't throw the baby out with the bath water. Survey your accomplishments. Why not take a moment right now and jot them down. A pencil is a great set of eyes.

Just because your "big" dream didn't turn out exactly like you planned doesn't mean that the many other dreams that did come true don't matter.

Just because you need a "new" dream to reenergize you now doesn't mean your life hasn't mattered. It has, and it will.

WHY DREAMS FAIL TO HATCH

Dreams sometimes fail to hatch because we have become myopic. We have lost the "big picture" of what God is trying to do in the world, or perhaps we never have known it at all.

A man wrote me about a statement I made in *The Seven Seasons of a Man's Life*. Here's what I said: "Try to make decisions based upon your priorities, not your pressures."

"How can I do that," he asked sincerely, "when the pressures and obligations of life are overwhelming—friends dying with cancer, rebellious children, temptation of worldly gadgets, a decaying society, daily needs like rent, kid's school functions (band and sports), leaking roofs, cars that won't run, etc., etc. They keep me from finding in-depth time to meditate and refocus on knowing God and myself so I can serve God and celebrate my gifts."

Sometimes I think we believe a dream is going to be a "big" thing or a "future" thing. Perhaps some of us need to dream about the "process" of living, and how God might be calling us to "interact" as a called person in the sufferings and needs of the people around us day to day.

Perhaps we, and the man who wrote me, could dream about how to comfort friends who are dying with cancer, or how to quiet and discipline rebellious children (a task for a truly patient saint), or "salt" society as a social or political worker, or touch the lives of children, landlords, roofers, car mechanics, and so on. Every singular experience is an opportunity to fulfill the dream of serving God and loving humanity. If we won't do the little that is before us, why should we expect God to give us a dream that requires even more responsibility?

FINDING A NEW DREAM

Let's suppose that your dream really is dead. How can you go about the business of finding a new dream?

This is perhaps the most thrilling and simultaneously painful part of our humanity—discovering that endeavor which will put fire in our belly and energy in our feet.

But a word of caution: It can take a long time to dream a new dream. The midlife slump is a time of pruning. God prunes every fruitful branch to make it even more fruitful. The point often missed is that in a season of pruning we have been "cut." We need a healing time. The important thing is to let the body, mind, and soul heal.

Perhaps the crux of the midlife experience is that God wants to purify his people. If this is true, and I believe it is (see Daniel 11:35), then whatever we go through and for however long is a blessing not a curse. In other words, it is the kindness of God to, at the halfway mark, squeeze out the erroneous thinking, the bad attitudes, and the residue of sinful habits.

Allow God to build everything into your life that he wants to build in and to purge everything out of your life that he wants to purge out. It is this very process of submitting to the loving blows that prepares us for the dream that is still to come.

FOCUS QUESTIONS

1. Have you felt the midlife experience is useless?
2. What was your dream during the first half of life? How has it turned out? As you pursued that dream, what other areas have suffered?
3. Why do you think dreams die?
4. How has God led your life? Has it been a single picture that has steadily become more clear? Or has it been more like a series of pictures that get torn up as new dreams come into focus? Has it been some other way? Explain your answer.
5. The big idea for this chapter is this: Because God is good, your life will not turn out like you plan. It will turn out better. Do you agree or disagree, and why?

THREE

A Raging Boredom—The Toll of Forty Years

The aftertaste of affluence is boredom.
MICHAEL NOVAK, *BUSINESS AS A CALLING*

A MAN IN HIS EARLY FIFTIES was planning to divorce his wife of thirty years. He said, "Everything I have touched in the last ten years has turned to (delete expletive)."

He went on to articulate a number of disappointing business ventures and a growing emotional distance from his wife. His life had become monotonous and boring, and he was filled with anger over the way things were turning out. He said, "I feel empty."

THE PROBLEM

raging, adj.—marked by turmoil and fury
boredom, n.—a tedious sameness; monotony

We each want to invest our lives for a worthy cause. Early in life we realize how important it is to identify interests and goals that absorb, engage, and stimulate our minds. In our culture those interests often revolve around making money, acquiring a reputation, and gaining influence.

Sometimes the only thing worse than not getting what you want is getting it. On reaching the age of forty-nine one man said, "I've achieved every worldly goal I've set. Frankly, I have everything I need. Yet, I find a void in my life." It is quite possible to get exactly what you want and be just as unhappy as though you didn't get any of it at all.

By the halfway point we realize the sickly, sallow gods of affluence, prestige, and power over-promised and under-delivered. Once those idols arrested our affections. Once they propelled us out of bed in the morning. No longer. Those of us who chased them have become bored.

Ed and Janet, a couple with no children, lived alone in a seven-thousand square foot home. The husband was depressed. His wife asked, "What's wrong with you? We have everything we could possibly want." He answered, "We don't have anything."

Financially you feel disillusioned. The tantalizing but disappointing idea that "money will make me happy" abandons most of us after twenty or more years of labor—win or lose. It was a goal that simply wasn't big enough to satisfy the deeper longings of our hearts. Only the poor can still cling to the illusion that money will make them happy.

Intellectually you feel tepid and unchallenged. You are doing the same things you have always done. You do them well. You do them quickly. But they simply don't return back to you what they once did. Once upon a time what you did was the most important calling on your life. Purpose has been fulfilled, or it has died. You feel stalled, aimless, directionless. Your zeal has turned into what Søren Kierkegaard called "useless passion."

Physically you feel worn out. One moment you feel listless, weary, exhausted, fatigued, and feeble. The next moment you find yourself annoyed, jaded, irked, or furious.

A struggling man who turned fifty wrote, "I lived through a crisis at forty by increased activity. The one at fifty has been a little harder to ignore."

Emotionally you feel like you're getting over the flu. Everything seems so futile. "Meaningless! Meaningless! Everything is meaningless; a chasing after the wind." You live in an emotional dumpster.

Your relationships are threadbare. You have focused on concealing how shallow and tenuous things have become. There is much hidden pain. A couple in their late forties were struggling after twenty-four years of marriage. I bumped into him one day and asked how things were going. With tears in his eyes he said, "She asked me for a divorce three days ago." Just then a man he knew approached from behind and tapped him on the shoulder. As though he had flipped a switch, his entire persona changed and he greeted the man warmly. There is no possibility the man could have known anything at all was wrong.

We fear our failures will become public knowledge. Walter Anderson, editor of *Parade* magazine, put it this way: "What will I do when they find out I'm me?"[1]

You find a thread of cynicism running through your conversations that wasn't there before. Chuck Daly, Hall of Fame NBA coach said, "A pessimist is an optimist with experience." You suspect Humpty Dumpty was pushed. Inertia has overtaken you. The only party you've been to recently is a pity party. It is the Midlife Slump. For you, it is a dark night of the soul.

SYMPTOMS OF BOREDOM

One day I was visiting on the phone with an old friend, John, a usually upbeat, highly successful executive. Even though he had just completed the most successful project of his career, he expressed extreme dissatisfaction with his current position. The general state of his life was fatigue and disequilibrium. He could not put his finger on the reason why, but his pain was real.

I asked him the following questions. Reflect on your own life as you read along.

- How many hours per week do you work?
- How long have you been doing that?
- Are you a workaholic?
- Are you overcalendarized?
- How much time off have you taken in the last three years?
- Do you have a hobby?
- How do you unwind?
- Can you rest?
- How would your wife rate your marriage?
- Are you exercising?
- How is your walk with God?
- If you could do anything what would that be?
- Are you having fun or just trying to get through it?
- Could you take a personal retreat?
- Are you willing to wait on the Lord?
- Are you using your spiritual gifts?
- Is your burnout clock ticking?

In his case, he told me he was working sixty hours per week, but called back a week later to say he had reviewed his calendar and it was actually more like seventy hours. He said he did not feel that he was a workaholic, but he had been working at this pace for four years and had sped up in recent months. He had not taken any vacation time in three years and did not have a hobby.

When asked, "How do you unwind?" he gave an insightful answer. He said, "I like to golf, and travel with my wife—but not with deadlines. Recently, I have begun to enjoy going to a beautiful, quiet place and just sitting on a bench. My wife and I have a spot at the shore we like a lot. We'll just go there, sit still, listen to the breakers, and watch the birds. It really does have a wonderful effect on me." Notice how this answer addresses the vacuum of the soul for beauty and quiet.

Imagine you are a plane that just crashed. An investigative team has just recovered your "black box" transponder from the wreckage. Suppose that from the beginning of your flight until final impact everything you said and thought was recorded. The team is looking for clues to understand why you crashed. Why not take some time and reflect on the cause of your crash—the source of your raging boredom.

MAKEOVER

Since 1978 I have chaired the Thanksgiving Leadership Prayer Breakfast in Orlando, of which I am also the founder. After the first twelve years I found my interest waned because of the routineness in putting the event together. I didn't completely lose interest, but neither was it an arrow through my heart. As a result, the attendance had leveled off.

Then one day in the early 1990s a fresh idea came to institute the "Leader of the Year" award." This "juiced" me up. Next, we added a "host committee" of well-known Christian leaders down the left margin of our letterhead. Attendance doubled. Then we started to honor our congressional and state legislators and to recognize outstanding student leaders from our area. Again, a surge.

Each of these new ideas incrementally rejuvenated me in my role as chair. My increased enthusiasm got me more involved. My increased involvement resulted in attendance starting to grow again. It may be that you can cure your boredom through some fresh ideas. What would give you a thrill in the roles where you feel bored? What kind of makeover can get you growing again?

CHANGEOVER

Sometimes a makeover will do. Other times we need a changeover.

In the early 1980s I set an overarching business goal to acquire and develop ten million square feet of commercial real estate by August 28, 1992, my twentieth anniversary of entering business.

This was an intoxicating vision that energized the men and women on our staff. Everything we did was focused on meeting this goal. We had it all laid out year by year. Whenever a new policy or procedure was needed we always tried to make a "ten million square feet" decision. In other words, we wanted a policy that would work for the moment, but also one that would work later when we had met the goal. It was the same with equipment purchases, software acquisitions, and hiring new people. We always tried to make ten million square feet decisions.

By 1985 I had become two people inside. On one hand, I loved the exhilaration, the thrill of the chase. But on the other hand, I also was finding another side of me that "yawned" at this goal. It slowly ceased to be the meaningful fuel to keep me stoked. At the age of thirty-six I had the first inklings of a new career calling. In 1987 at the age of thirty-nine I sensed a distinct call to change careers. The boredom was raging. However, it was not until early 1991 that I actually made a move. Six years. It took a long time to make the move, but I couldn't be happier now.

Sometimes we must engage our boredom with questions to understand it. Sometimes we must accept our boredom with patience until we hear God's voice. Sometimes we must embrace our boredom, realizing it is a husk that when blown away will leave a new, better calling. Do you see a changeover in your future?

ATTACKING THE ROOTS OF BOREDOM

Where has boredom attacked you? Is it in your relationship with your mate? Have you lost your vocational passion? Or is it a broader, more vague, pervasive, generalized boredom?

To get at the root of your boredom, work through the Focus Questions, considering the following major relationships and activities.

FOCUS QUESTIONS

1. How bored are you in your relationship with God?

   - Why do you feel that way?
   - Why can you have hope?
   - What is one positive step you can take this week to makeover this relationship?

2. How bored are you in your relationship with your wife?

   - Why do you feel that way?
   - Why can you have hope?
   - What is one positive step you can take this week to makeover this relationship?

3. How bored are you in your relationships with your children and/or grandchildren?

   - Why do you feel that way?
   - Why can you have hope?
   - What is one positive step you can take this week to makeover these relationships?

4. How bored are you in your vocation?

   - Why do you feel that way?
   - Why can you have hope?
   - What is one positive step you can take this week to makeover or changeover this area?

5. How bored are you in your church?

   - Why do you feel that way?
   - Why can you have hope?
   - What is one positive step you can take this week to makeover or changeover this area?

6. How bored are you in your personal ministry?

- Why do you feel that way?
- Why can you have hope?
- What is one positive step you can take this week to makeover or changeover this area?

7. How bored are you with your community involvement?

- Why do you feel that way?
- Why can you have hope?
- What is one positive step you can take this week to makeover or changeover this area?

8. How bored are you with what you do for recreation and health?

- Why do you feel that way?
- Why can you have hope?
- What is one positive step you can take this week to makeover or changeover this area?

9. How bored are you with your investments and money management?

- Why do you feel that way?
- Why can you have hope?
- What is one positive step you can take this week to makeover or changeover this area?

10. How bored are you with _____?

- Why do you feel that way?
- Why can you have hope?
- What is one positive step you can take this week to makeover or changeover this area?

FOUR

An Uninvited Paunch— Embracing the Bulge

I would feel a lot more middle-aged if I knew more ninety-year-olds!

A FRIEND, ON TURNING FORTY-FIVE

ONE EVENING I TOOK PATSY TO see the movie *Sense and Sensibility*. We arrived at the theater plenty early, but Patsy surprised me when she said, "The movie isn't posted on the marquee. It looks like that movie isn't playing here."

One fortunate advantage of midlife is that we're not so quick to make fools of ourselves.

If I had still been in my twenties my immediate response would have been, "Well, I don't care what the marquee says, I know I'm right." And then I would have argued with the ticket clerk that there must be some kind of mistake.

If I had still been between thirty and forty-five I would have toned it down and said, "Well, I think I'm right . . . but I could be wrong." By then I was willing to confess, at least privately, that I occasionally made mistakes.

Instead, since I am beyond forty-five, I gave my now standard answer, "Well, I'm probably wrong . . . but I could be right!" Just then I remembered the movie was actually playing at a different theater about two blocks away. Since we had been early we hot-footed over there with time to spare.

Recently, after I shared this story, a man who had hit sixty said if it had been him, his response would have been, "Okay. I know I'm wrong. Now if I can just remember why!"

And then a man in his seventies told me he would say, "Who cares!"

THE PROBLEM

By the middle years we're each trying to cope with a litany of "reductions" to our beauty, brains, and brawn. We have been deteriorating all along, of course, but by the midpoint it's hard to ignore the cumulative effect.

A friend pointed out how peer group pool parties tell an interesting tale. When the parents of small children have their pool parties they all show up in sleek, (disgustingly) tanned bodies. All the guys pump iron. The women look anorexic. Those kids are really proud of those bodies! (Show-offs).

When seniors go to pool parties they let it all hang out. They have passed the age of caring about what everyone thinks. They just dive in and have a great time—like they did when they were little kids.

How about middle-agers? Basically, we don't go to pool parties. I know personally I would rather walk through the mall in a tutu than take my shirt off for a swim around peers. My skin color matches the whites of my eyes.

During the middle years we each go through a host of vanities about our beloved bodies. It's ironic. When we were younger we looked at older people and thought, "They're cool!" We were even intimidated by their experience and age. Now that we ourselves are older we look at younger people and think, "They're cool!" Now we can even get intimidated by their perfect hair and teeth and feel inferior.

In the early stages of the "maturing" of our minds and bodies we focus on trying to defeat nature. We run; we diet; we get tanned. Then in early midlife we shift to disguises. It's a cover-up with clothing and dyes. Later, when we finally make peace with our aging, most of us shift from beating to embracing the bulge.

Some problems are more serious. A middle-aged man lost the sight in his left eye. A middle-aged woman had a cancerous breast removed. A few of our friends and acquaintances have died prematurely and confronted us with our own mortality.

The physical and mental problems of today's "old" people didn't exist that long ago because people didn't live long enough to get Alzheimer's or some of the cancers.

Perhaps the greatest challenge comes to the changing relationship of husband and wife. How does a husband bombarded by a youth- and sex-saturated society relate to a wife who is desperately trying to postpone the aging process or, alternately, has given up? How does a wife respond to a husband whose sexual drive is slowing down at the same time his hair loss is speeding up?

Here's a comforting idea you can organize your philosophy around: Because God is good, every imperfect body has been made imperfect in a perfect way.

TWO LARGE, LOOMING QUESTIONS

We each want to feel good about ourselves. As we age, the great question to ask about our changing bodies and forgetful minds is, "What's normal?" In others words, what's the average?

Our task is to resolve the tension between our "expectations" and what "is." If we can get a handle on "what's normal" then we can have reasonable expectations of ourselves.

The other great question is, "What should I expect from my mate?"

To successfully negotiate this passage we must be patient. We must let changing physical realities "season" our expectations. When your body or mind or the body or mind of your mate starts to lose its supple "youth," give yourself at least a couple of years to adjust your expectations.

What are the changes that are taking place?

The Body

I knew irrevocably that I was middle-aged the day someone in my Sunday school class asked for prayer for their hemorrhoids (yes, this really did happen).

Sylvester "Rocky" Stallone once reigned as the cultural icon of physical fitness. After gaining thirty pounds for a movie role, the body-building Stallone acknowledged how much vanity goes into it. He admits he cried on his fiftieth birthday. "That made me reach for the Xanax. It's a nightmare. When you're younger, you think you're going to live forever. Twenty years is so far away. But twenty years is really just a speed bump when you reach the middle of life."

What's happening physically at midlife?

While strolling on the Disney World Boardwalk one evening, Patsy and I stopped to watch the eyes of a four-year-old dance with amazement and wonder as he stood in front of one of those wavy mirrors that distort your body. Little does he know. . . .

The main feature at this stage of life is a relocation of body parts due to a long association with gravity. It would be depressing if it wasn't so funny, and it would be funny if it wasn't so depressing!

We start out in all shapes and sizes, and we inevitably end up in worse shapes and bigger sizes. This is the season when you diet and gain weight.

The Mind

Remember when you used to pride yourself on your good memory? If you're like me, now you can't remember why.

My wife, a staunch Nutrasweet user, started her irreversible journey toward becoming more forgetful about the time rumors were flying that Nutrasweet causes a loss in short-term memory. So whenever she would forget something I would ask her, "Have you been taking Nutrasweet today?"

"I can't remember," she would deadpan back.

While long-term memory tends to remain good, short-term memory becomes an oxymoron. One evening I was in a hotel room preparing to go downstairs to a dinner and give a speech. I fell into a terrible panic when I couldn't find my glasses anywhere. Finally, I said to myself, "Okay, now, calm down. Think. Where could you have put them?"

As I sat down on the bed to think it over, I heard a nauseating crunch.

A useful by-product of our forgetfulness is a new humility. We tend not to think so highly of ourselves and, when we do that, we open ourselves up to learn from others in a fresh way.

Clothing

Early in life we purchase clothing to feature our figure or physique. By midlife the purpose of clothing has changed from emphasis to concealment.

During the first years of the midlife experience we keep letting out our clothes. Each passing year we leave another embarrassing mark on our belts as our waistlines expand.

Now, many of our favorite suits simply don't fit. But we love those clothes, and are not about to give them away! One day, circa age forty, we notice a thick coat of dust across the shoulders of those treasured garments. Finally, it sinks in: "You will never wear those duds again." You begin building a new wardrobe in the new size. So what happens to the old clothes? A story will explain.

A friend of mine, Eric, wears the unusual suit size of 42 long. One day he drove by a garage sale with a sign out front advertising 42 long suits. He couldn't believe it! He pulled over, and bought several expensive suits in brand-new condition for a few dollars apiece. The former owner, who had finally hit forty, decided to give it up.

The Face

It's a downer day to realize those hairline cracks in the mirror are really your face. The first half of life carves its mark on our faces— creases, furrows, wrinkles, spots, sags, tags, drooping dimples, or double chins.

Our faces start to look permanently the way we have repeatedly made them look temporarily. In my own case, my eyes are light sensitive, plus I get intense when I'm focusing on a task. So I tend to knot my brow. As a result of the repeated temporary furrowing of my brow, I now have a permanent, vertical valley above my nose between my eyebrows.

I will not soon forget the day I first became unhappy with this furrow. I would stare at it for long periods. I would try to contort my face so it would go away. I would practice relaxing. I became quite self-conscious of it and was sure people were focusing in on this part of my face and staring at it. This went on for a couple of years, after which I realized I couldn't do anything about it and learned to accept it. Now I don't think about it at all.

I believe we each go through a series of these stunning revelations about our faces and other body parts. I remember developing a couple of "tags"—those little random growths around the face. I couldn't see anything else in the mirror for months. Eventually, I had them cut off. And did I ever feel better!

The Hair

Someone jotted me this note: "Midlife is the metallic age. We get silver in our hair, gold in our teeth, and lead in our bottom."

The only problem with silver hair is that it makes you look old. The other day I looked around at all the middle-aged women in our church. Remember the old commercial, "Only your hairdresser will know for sure"? That's not true. I know. They are all highlighting or coloring their hair.

But at least they have hair. While women are figuring out which color to use, men are trying to figure out how to glue it back onto the scalp. This is the season when most men's hair begins to thin out. If it doesn't thin out evenly, it attacks the little spot where a yarmulke might go. Or as speaker Crawford Loritts says of his receding hairline, "Every year I have more face to wash."

The irony of hair care is that the less you have the more time it requires.

I will forever remember the mornings in my early forties when I would sit at the desk in my study and literally pull out handfuls of hair. I figured for sure that I would be bald like my grandfather within a year. Then, after advancing a couple of inches north, it suddenly stopped dropping. At least I don't have to worry about that cowlick anymore.

While women pretend only their hairdressers know, men make secret telephone inquiries to the Rogaine 800 number and drive across town to a drugstore so they can read a "Just for Men" box without bumping into anyone they know.

The Eyes

In my high school black horn-rimmed glasses were the "in" thing. Most of us had a pair—a few of us actually needed them. In my case, I had plain glass lenses.

In my twenties I actually developed a need for glasses, but by then I didn't want them. So I opted for contact lenses. I always told people that it was because the contacts were so much more compatible with all the sports I played. A lie. The real reason was cosmetic.

In my thirties I remember thinking how much more mature I would look for business purposes if I wore reading glasses. For several years I recall disappointment when my optometrist said, "No, not yet." Reading glasses are crutches for eyes. As we age our corneas become more brittle and can no longer make the adjustment for close viewing. Rule of thumb: If you don't know whether or not you need reading glasses—you don't!

In my forties, because of allergies, I started to get bags under my eyes, so I switched to glasses to dampen the effect of saggy, baggy eyes. Today, in my late forties, I've lost all my shame because I don't even seem to care if my glasses are on crooked.

Oh, and how about those squirrelly eyebrows?

The Teeth

Many people in the middle years have turned to what Gail Sheehy calls "teeth things."

For some of us in this season, we watch our teeth "wander" in different directions over a couple of decades. More and more, midlifers are getting braces.

The Skin

Have you ever looked at your mate's skin and thought you were sitting next to your mother? It happens. But for a reality check, look at your own skin.

The Ears

A lot of baby boomers are saying, "Huh?"

Rock and roll damage has left a lot of midlifers out of the conversation. As we age it becomes more and more difficult to individuate sounds. That's why it's so hard to make out table conversation in a noisy restaurant. All the sounds run together.

One type of damage is tinnitus, a perpetual ringing in the ears. For others of us, loud music destroys our ability to hear certain frequencies. For example, I can hear the alarm on my wristwatch out of one ear, but not the other.

But what's really annoying are those little hairs growing out of our ears!

Energy

Energy management becomes a real issue sometime in the forties. We can no longer skip breaks and eat at our desks. To be an effective person beyond the forties is to develop a personal system to manage our energy. This might include improved diet, weight loss, naps, vitamins, and exercise.

Jim and Marge, friends of ours, slip on walking shoes and take early-morning walks together around their neighborhood. Personally, I row a one-man scull most every day on the lake behind our home. If you have felt your energy flagging, maybe it's time to reengineer your schedule and habits. Many who have done so find lethargy giving way to feeling twenty years younger.

CONCLUSION

You and I cannot postpone the effects of time—not really. By all means do everything you want to be fit and remain youthful. On the other hand, let's relax and enjoy our middle-agedness. If it's profitable to make Barbie dolls that look more "normal," how much more profitable to our well-being to accept our changing minds and bodies as normal.

FOCUS QUESTIONS

1. What is it about the physical part of turning middle-aged that has upset you, and why?
2. What should we consider "normal" for our midpoint minds? our midlife bodies?
3. If you are married, how have the changes in your mate affected you? Have your expectations been reasonable or not, and why?

4. What are the changes you've experienced in each of the following areas, and how have you reacted to those changes?

- Your mind
- Your clothing
- Your face
- Your hair
- Your eyes
- Your teeth
- Your skin
- Your ears
- Your energy

FIVE

The Shrinking Nest—Coping
with the Loss

*It will be gone before you know it. The fingerprints on
the wall appear higher and higher. Then, suddenly,
they disappear.*

DOROTHY EUSLIN

MY WIFE'S COUSIN, CHARLIE, AND HIS wife have two precious children. After graduation from college their oldest, a boy, became engaged.

Though Charlie is a psychiatrist by profession, he is also an ordained minister. So he performed the wedding ceremony for his son and the bride.

Before the bride and groom entered the church, Charlie stood before those assembled to extend a welcome. As his eyes panned the large congregation he flashed a broad, warm smile to each of us. He paused, as though searching for what to say next, then said, "Where did the time go?"

Isn't this the question every parent ponders?

THE PROBLEM

A few months ago my wife, our eighteen-year-old son, and I were sitting together in a little diner where we would share our last meal together. Within a few hours we would separate. John would go in one direction to the exhilarating new world of college. Patsy and I would drive off in the other direction toward an empty home filled with the aggreeable ghosts of many happy memories.

As we embraced on last time I said, "John, this is a moment for which you are well prepared." And it was true. It was a moment for which Patsy and I, on the other hand, were not. No amount of forethought and preparation could prepare us for the sadness.

One mother said, "After we dropped off our son at college I cried all the way home, and I couldn't stop crying." Dads cry, too.

A child leaving home creates an emotional flood. Perhaps it's off to college, or taking a first job and setting up an apartment. For our departing child it's a time of raw excitement, mixed with a pinch of trepidation. We want to "be there" for them—to provide all the emotional support and encouragement they need.

However, while we want to "be strong" for them, this change touches us just as much as them. There is one major difference, however. For our child it is a great, robust, expansive season of "gain" with a dash of "loss." For us, though, it is often the other way around. The sense of loss outweighs the sense of gain—at least initially.

So while we want to enter into the pleasure felt by our departing child, we must also cope with our own emotions—alternating surges of salty tears and robust laughter, sadness and happiness, regret and joy, disappointment and satisfaction, fear and hope, confidence and anxiety.

Other times this experience becomes tragic. When our next-door neighbor's two daughters went off to college the husband said, "That phase of my life is over. There's really no purpose left for us to be married." A few months later he left to live with another woman.

MOTHERS

One of the kindest acts a man can offer his wife as the nest empties is to understand what she goes through. Basically, mothers worry. A mother said, "No matter how far away they move or how often you see them, you will never stop worrying about their well-being."

Mothers and fathers have different "issues" to work through as the nest starts to empty. Essentially, if they do their work well, mothers work themselves out of a job. The emptying nest is a far greater emotional event for a mother than a father—though fathers can get really strung out.

Even greater than the emotional impact, though, is the practical impact. She becomes unemployed in one of her major life roles.

Every mother will have thought about this in advance, of course. For mothers already employed outside the home (seventy-five percent are), then this becomes an opportunity to further excel in their work. It may be a season to explore additional training or a new field, part-time or full-time.

Work-at-home mothers will have a larger transition to make. Short of nursery work, working in a day-care center, or grandchildren to watch, she will fill her hours, for income or as a volunteer, with labor that will require some new training or retraining. Statistically, few women actually enter the job market as the nest empties.[1] Those who do go "back to work" must cope with a lot of stress. Husbands, this is a season to be extra gentle and supportive.

FATHERS

By nature mothers "nurture" more than fathers. While there are exceptions, most men have not been the primary caregivers to their children.

On the other hand, the bond of love between fathers and their children is so strong that dads feel the loss just as deeply as moms, though it is customary to conceal such feelings.

Patsy and I are at the stage when many of our friends are dropping their firstborn child off at college. Several fathers have in essence said, "The hardest thing I've ever had to do is drop off my first child at college."

While both moms and dads can have regrets, it is often the fathers who are most pierced by the "if onlys" and "I wish I would haves." This can create a lot of anxiety for a man. Let your wife know that this is a season in which you will need her help to process your regrets. Remember, though, that your hard work was not only necessary, but also provided the economic "fuel" that kept your family running.

THE NEST EMPTIES

The day your children spread their wings and take flight is a day of reckoning. In one sense, an "accounting" is taken of our stewardship with each child. Were we faithful? Was there anything major left undone? Our "payday" comes when we feel good about our answers.

It's ironic. Once the impact of the departing moment subsides, both child and parent come to realize that they both have gained a greater sense of freedom.

There are different kinds of nests. Let's look them over.

Shrinking Nest

The nest doesn't empty out all at once. When our daughter, Jen, left for college she left her brother behind.

Yes, it was a huge adjustment to make, but having John around meant the house wasn't completely empty.

The biggest change I've noticed is how much I'm concentrating on making an investment in our son for the remaining time before he, too, goes off. In fact, I have intentionally set a goal that I have called "focusing on the nest." In other words, he'll be gone in one year so I want to spend as much time with him as he feels comfortable giving me. Much of this involves attending his events. Recently I went to watch him play in a "pick up" basketball game that didn't mean a thing. He actually discouraged me from going, but I could tell he was glad I went anyway. Sometimes I'll go lie on his bed and "hang out" while he's experimenting on the Internet.

The last few years before a teenager leaves home can require a lot of patience and imagination. Boys especially don't give much feedback on what's happening in their lives—and when they do, they mumble!

One Sunday morning we were getting ready for church. Patsy was in the kitchen with John, and I was in the bedroom getting dressed. Patsy rushed in and said, "Get out there! John's talking!" We smiled at each other, I stopped tying my tie, and went into the kitchen for ten minutes of listening to John wax enthusiastically about a broad range of topics of interest to him.

Experimental Empty Nest

We have also been going through a phenomenon that I have been calling "experimental empty nest."

On several occasions John has spent the night with a friend, gone on a class trip, attended a church retreat, or been away at a sports camp. For blocks of several days at a time we find ourselves in a strangely quiet home.

Experimental empty nest has been good because it allows us to take "empty nesting" out for a trial spin. Actually, it's kind of nice, especially when the boy comes back home!

Empty Nest

Ned and Kathy's son announced he was getting married. In earnest they tried to talk him into waiting. "He was so young," said Kathy.

But he wouldn't have any part of it, so they gave him their blessing. After the ceremony the bride and groom drove off into the sunset. Ned and Kathy walked to their van, got in, looked at each other, and simultaneously said, "Yes!" as they gave each other a high five.

Someone has said the most beautiful lights are tail lights.

Once the transition has been negotiated—the wife's "unemployment" and the husband's regrets—most couples find they truly enjoy the empty nest. It is a season of rediscovering each other. Now there is "time"—lots of it—to do those things that you've always said you'd like to try.

Dave and Claudia Arp surveyed five hundred people for their book *The Second Half of Marriage*. Interestingly, what people forty through forty-nine most looked forward to for their marriages in the future was "more time" (thirty-two percent). In contrast, what people fifty through fifty-nine (who had more time) most looked forward to for their marriages in the future was "companionship" (forty-nine percent).[2]

Revolving Nest

Today's mixed families mean that some couples in second marriages may have one set of younger children and one or more sets of older children. One woman said, "Allen has older, married children with families of their own. I have younger kids. Between his kids, mine, and the grandchildren I don't think there will ever be a time when we are truly an empty nest!"

Many couples are finding that the path for many of their kids is "in and out and back in again." "Boomerang" children live at home after college. The economics of our times, corporate restructurings, and divorcing children have led to an entirely new cultural phenomenon of adult children moving back in with their parents for short and long stays.

Expanding Nest

Phil had been on the road most of the week. That was normal. And so was phoning home daily to see how his wife, eighteen-year-old daughter, and fifteen-year-old son were doing.

After one particularly long week, Phil called on Thursday evening to say he was flying out the next morning to come home. After the usual exchange his wife mentioned Kelly, their daughter, had some important news to share with him when he arrived. He tried to pull it out of them, but it was useless.

On the plane home he did a lot of thinking about Kelly. She was a good kid, active in their church youth group. She had just graduated from high school and planned to attend a local college. She was dating a young man but had told Phil and his wife they were just good friends. She had made a commitment to keep herself for the husband God would give her.

When Phil arrived he anxiously asked, "What's this so-called important news?" His daughter, Kelly, burst into tears and blurted out three words he never thought he would hear from his unmarried daughter: "Dad, I'm pregnant."

Phil was speechless. He just sat there. He didn't know what to say or do. He was thinking, *How could she do this to us? What was she thinking? What are people going to say? I can't wait to get my hands on that no-good boy. God, why would you let this happen to me?*

He was lost in a trance of self-pity when he heard his wife yelling, "Phil! Phil! Aren't you going to say anything? Say something!"

He couldn't. He sat immobile while his daughter continued to sob. Then he sensed that God was trying to get his attention. Phil later said, "I think he was yelling, 'Phil! Phil! Aren't you going to say anything? Say something!'"

He thought, *God, I don't know what to say. I don't know what to do. You know this is not in my five-year plan! This is not supposed to happen to my family—my daughter. God, I'm ticked! Where did I go wrong?*

At that moment Phil heard God speak plainly to his inner spirit: "Show to your daughter—My daughter—what I have shown to you. Say to your daughter—My daughter—what I have said to you time after time in your past and will continue to say in your future."

He began to weep. He knew what he needed to do. He wrapped his arms around his daughter, pulled her close, and said, "Kelly, there is a Father in heaven who has forgiven you and loves you unconditionally. And there is a father here on earth who forgives and loves you unconditionally, too."

Phil and his wife committed themselves to reflect the grace, forgiveness, and unconditional love of God to their daughter. Kelly confessed her sin to God and her parents that day. She also understood the consequences of her sin. The young man made it clear he wanted nothing to do with the baby or Kelly. They haven't seen him since. Not long after that, Kelly gave birth to a healthy eight-pound, nine-ounce baby girl.

Phil reports it has not been easy. There have been many tearful moments. One morning Kelly asked her father, "Dad, will any man ever want to marry me?"

Phil said, "I pondered what she was asking and I believe God gave me the words. He said, 'Tell her I never say, "oops!"' That morning I couldn't assure her that a man would marry her, but I could assure her of a faithful God who never, ever says oops!"

Phil reminded her that since God knows the beginning from the end, he knew and even allowed this to happen. "Before the foundation of this world God has orchestrated your life. You can put your past, your present, and your future in his care because he cares for you. You can put your trust completely in him because he is never, ever surprised by what happens, and he never says oops!" (Kelly recently married a fine young man who loves both her and her child.)

OPPORTUNITIES

Whether you are in a shrinking nest, an empty nest, a revolving nest, or an expanding nest, God has orchestrated your life. You can rest in the knowledge that he never says oops! What happens may not be how you would have scripted your five-year plan, but God is good.

Most of us will end up sitting in an empty nest. After the initial jolt, an eventual readjustment takes place. You will have newfound freedom and time. How have other people used it? Here are some areas to think about:

- Reinvent your marriage (see chapter 19)
- Develop new or old hobbies, interests, avocations—especially ones you can do as a couple
- Develop a personal ministry
- Take up golf, tennis, or some other sport
- Take a daily walk or other exercise
- Go back to school
- Learn how to use a computer and the Internet
- Take vocational training or retraining
- Change careers
- Become a community volunteer
- Teach a Sunday school class
- Move to a new home
- Move to a new city
- Become a foster parent
- Mentor a teen

What other ideas can you think of? Why not make a list of the top five things you would like to do in the empty nest phase.

If you're married, talk these over with your mate. What are things you can do together? Give it a try. You may have to go to your number 3, 4, or 5 to find a mutual interest, but it will be well worth the effort.

FOCUS QUESTIONS

1. "Where did the time go?" What comes to mind when you ponder this question?
2. Do you have a shrinking nest, an "experimental" empty nest, an empty nest, a revolving nest, or an expanding nest? Whatever your situation, what is the opportunity it represents?
3. If your children have left the home, how has your wife coped? If you still have children in the home, have you been talking to your

wife about the transition? What one thing can you do to show her your love and support today?

4. As men, we tend to be the ones peirced with regrets. Yet, providing is a noble contribution to the process of raising a family. What are your feelings about the empty nest? Do you need to give yourself a little more credit? Or do you need to forgive yourself, ask for forgiveness, and move on?

5. Did you make a list of the top five things you would like to do in the empty-nest phase? If not, do it now. Next, make an "appointment" with your wife, and begin to dream about the things you might do together.

S I X

A Stumbling Career—Dealing with Getting or Not Getting What We Want

All people seek happiness. This is without exception. . . . This is the motive of every action of every man, even of those who hang themselves.

BLAISE PASCAL, *PENSEES*

AVID HAS BEEN SEARCHING FOR A fresh sense of meaning for his life. For several years he has felt "stuck" in a career rut. Recently we were talking about his work when another man—not knowing our topic—walked up and said, "How's the job going?"

David tensed and glanced down, weighing how truthful to be, then said, "Well, it keeps the bills paid." He tried to put a good face on it, but the tense jaw and the worried eyes betrayed him.

Larry recently said, "Pat, my walk with God is strong, my marriage has never been better, my company is just coming off the most profitable year in our history . . . but I've lost my passion. I just don't feel the fire anymore."

THE PROBLEM

Every career stumbles in its own way. Some stumble in a highly visible way; others stumble on the "inside" where no one knows. It would surprise me if you identify with everything I'm about to say, but much of it may put into words what you've been feeling.

A universal motive inspires every graduating student: "I want to do something with my life."

The graduate is looking for some sort of calling or vision to be a "change agent"—to leave the world a better place, to make a mark, to leave some fingerprints on history. This is usually expressed in terms of a vocation or career.

As the graduate enters the working world, however, the same economic forces that forge a robust economy also shape this person's lifestyle values. Ask a man in his early thirties why he works and he will likely reply, "I want to improve my family's standard of living."

Notice the not-so-subtle change from "I want to do something with my life" to "I want to improve my family's standard of living." This is a dramatic shift in our basic motivation from production to consumption. This has a far-reaching impact on what we "give ourselves to" during the first half of our productive lives.

We start out to be producers but quickly become consumers, too. Here's the problem. As we pursue these two dreams—making a difference and living well—we become "encumbered." We tend to live up to the limits of our means. The lifestyle looks good, but at the price of an enormous amount of energy—physical, mental, and emotional.

Then sometime in our thirties, forties, or fifties "it" happens. Suddenly the pressure starts to get to you. You dread the deadlines that once intoxicated you. You find yourself procrastinating. You do not find joy and pleasure in tasks that were once your mainstay—even your trademark. You start thinking, "Been there, done that, have the T-shirt." You're just not motivated.

Maybe you achieved your goal, maybe not. It doesn't make any difference. The thrill is gone. You're on auto-pilot. Either you have gone as far as you can where you are—you're "under" employed—or the job has gotten too big for you—you're "over" employed. It doesn't matter. You've played the game and, win or lose, you're tired of the rules, the games, the repetition. You're experiencing frustration rather than fulfillment. You have hit the wall or can feel yourself hurtling toward it.

You begin to wonder, *Is this who I really am?* You've been at it so long that the line between your job description (what you do) and your personal identity (who you are) has blurred.

You're bored. You need or want a new challenge. You feel like your boss (if you have one) has not helped you celebrate your giftedness. You are using all of your energy but not all of your capacity.

You feel like you are being consumed. You feel you have more to offer. You would like a new opportunity to showcase what you can really do.

This compelling desire animates not just senior managers but all managers. Michael Novak, in *Business As a Calling*, says,

> Being a middle manager is not primarily a way station on the way to the top. Probably everyone wants at first to test themselves against that possibility; but, realistically, most middle managers expect some advancement . . . while expecting to remain middle managers until retirement. Middle management, many know early, is their calling. They want to be super good at it. They want to make a contribution. Most of all, they need to know in their own minds that they have done so.[1]

You sense deep within you a longing to do something of substance. You want your life to make a difference. You want it to matter that you have walked the face of this planet. In essence, you want to return to your original compelling motive: "I want to do something with my life." You need a new vision.

But because you have been such a "consumer" you have "mortgaged" your future. You have financial responsibilities. While you are coming into your peak earning years, you are also in, or coming into, your peak spending years—college educations, a bigger mortgage to go along with the bigger income, and a bigger car payment to reflect your increased status. You feel stuck. You have heard about people your age who found themselves unemployable or had to take a huge "hit" in income. It makes you shudder.

How would you answer the following questions right now?

1. Did you get what you wanted?
2. Has it made you happy?
3. Do you want to make a change?

The rest of this chapter and Chapter 20, "Midlife Career Changes—Or Renewing the Career You Already Have," will address the issues raised by these questions.

Shifting Values

I remember the day in my early thirties when theologian R. C. Sproul[2] asked me if there was some core value underlying my work as a real estate developer.

Without hesitating I said, "Competence. I love anything done well." Then, I proceeded to tell him how I had admired a street sweeper I once saw at Disney World. With broom in hand he put his all into his work— he flipped those cigarette butts into his scooper forward and backward! He did it with such flair that he truly became part of the show.

It would be difficult to find one word to sum up the first half of our productive adult lives, but if we could select only one I believe it would be "competence."

During the first half of your productive life you pursued (and admired) competence, achievement, and accomplishment—getting things done and done well. It was a high value for you—still is. It's what drove you to pursue excellence in your work. It's what you have appreciated in others.

You're pretty good at what you do. You have a reputation. But now you have reached a plateau. You spent fifteen, twenty, twenty-five, or more years perfecting this competence. You went full tilt for it. But competence has lost its motivational "force."

You don't want to jettison the values that got you here. But your intuition tells you that those values alone are not enough to finish the race.

It would be equally difficult to find one word to sum up the desire for the second half, but if we could choose only one I believe it would be "substance." In other words, we want what we do to actually "mean something." This change of value applies equally to those who believe they have been "successful" and those who do not.

I have gathered a number of ideas under the category of substance: meaning, purpose, sense of contribution, and making a difference in the world. The following chart compares a few values for the first and second halves. Which values propelled you during the first half? Are there others? Which ones do you believe will most energize you for the second half of your journey? Can you think of others?

First Half:	Second Half:
Competence	Substance
Consumption	Contribution
Performance	Meaning
Success	Success that matters
Achievement	Significance
Goals	Purpose
Action	Peace
Results	Beauty
Efficiency	Aesthetics

Of course, moving toward second-half values doesn't mean abandoning what was right in the first half. Some of us will only need to fine-tune ourselves. Others, though, will need to jettison the wrong-minded values that have ground progress to a halt. In any event, everyone will make some changes in the core values that motivate their work.

Finding Your "Vacuum of the Soul"

It started for me at age thirty-six (the early side) and it can occur well into your midfifties. (Remember, in our diverse culture there is no singular midlife experience anymore). You come to a point that you feel somehow imbalanced—like something is missing, like it's not enough. All the years of pressure deadlines and making the "nut" have taken a toll. You have discovered a vacuum in your soul for meaning, beauty, and quiet.

Today I realize that R. C. Sproul probably expected to hear me say my core value was "beauty," because we built beautiful buildings. I didn't though, because I had never taken time to enjoy them. That's why I developed a vacuum in my soul for beauty. Now I am virtually obsessed with admiring and appreciating beauty, especially in nature and all its interwoven ecosystems. Where have you been "out of balance"? Where do you feel the vacuum? There's no reason why you can't also begin to "shift" your values to compensate for the years of neglect.

MOTIVATED ABILITIES

At the midpoint many of us must come to grips with the simple fact that we are not a "fit" for our work, or at least large portions of our job. This, after we have invested as much as two decades into a career. Here is a useful device from People Management in Connecticut to help you evaluate whether or not you "fit" your present vocation.

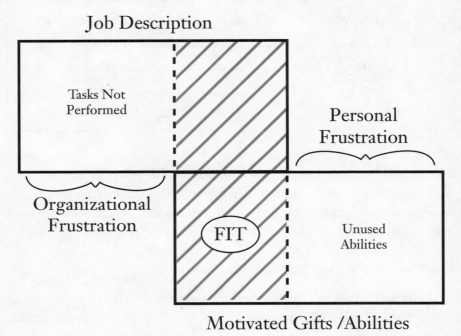

Figure 1.1

In Figure 1.1 the top box represents your job description, and the bottom box represents your motivated abilities. One represents what the organization needs; the other represents what you enjoy and are "good at"—what you need.

The shaded area represents where there is a "fit." In this case there is not a complete fit. What does this mean?

This produces two unhappy results. First, the employer experiences organizational frustration because the employee doesn't perform major responsibilities or does so poorly.

Second, the employee experiences personal frustration because a portion of his or her motivated abilities go untapped.[3]

What happens when there is not a fit? I have been amazed over the years at how people figure out how to do (and not do) what they want—even when you pay their salary! People do exactly what they want to do—what they are motivated to do.

In short, when the job description and motivated abilities don't "line up," the employee will do that portion of the job description that motivates him and leave the rest undone (or at least procrastinate). This, of course, frustrates the organization. Just as frustrating, but for the individual, a significant portion of his or her motivated abilities and skill set goes unused.

When there is a strong fit between your job description and motivated abilities you will be happy in your work. It will look like Figure 1.2.

Make a written list of your motivated abilities—things you do well that you enjoy. Now take a copy of your job description (or make one if you don't already have one in writing) and evaluate how motivated you are to do each responsibility and duty. If you find that many of your tasks don't really turn your crank, you may have isolated why you are no longer happy. You may need to renegotiate your job description or make a move.

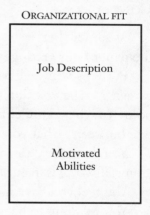

Figure 1.2

SPECIAL CHALLENGES FOR MINORITIES

The most successful minorities are those who have best adapted to the majority white-Anglo-European culture of business, government, law, medicine, the arts, education, and so on. That is changing.

Several decades of legal integration has led to a professional integration. Younger whites who have grown up with men and women of color are more likely to see someone for "the content of their character rather than the color of their skin." The dream is coming true in many respects.

Undeniably the "glass ceiling" of color remains. One black man in a southern city put it all on the line during a racial reconciliation meeting. He said, "If you look at the top one hundred privately owned businesses in this city, not one of them is black owned or has a black chief executive.

So let's get something clear: Either we are an inferior people, or something else is going on."

Something else has been going on, but I believe blacks and other minorities are today where women were in the 1970s. In the next twenty-five years, we will undoubtedly see black success stories move from exception to normative. Indeed, we can already see the first ripples.

As African Americans and other people of color reach midlife, their struggle is likely to be one of a continuing struggle for "a place at the table." During your half-time, by God's grace, you will find second wind to continue the struggle.

CONCLUSION

As said earlier, every career stumbles in its own way. Only you know the pain of not getting what you wanted.

Perhaps you feel you have already passed the high point of your career. Maybe you don't feel like your career has ever even had a high point. Maybe your identity has taken a beating. Perhaps you blurred the line between "what you do" and "who you are" and then were dumped.

You don't feel "valuable" or as valuable as you did in the beginning. Your self-worth is in question. You're tired. You're bored. You're frustrated.

You feel you have more to offer. You do.

You're going to be just fine.

Midlife is a season. It is a season when core values shift from competence to substance. It is a season to "match up" our motivated abilities with a job we can love. It is the season when we learn how to fill the vacuum of our soul for beauty and peace.

Soon, if not already, you will be ready for a new challenge. You will find yourself animated once again by that original compelling motive: "I want to do something with my life." You will want (and by God's grace, find) a position in which you can showcase your gifts.

Your energy will rebound. One man, seventy-two, told me, "I feel like I am thirty years younger than I look in the mirror!"

The second half promises to be a vibrant, fulfilling season. You will stumble, perhaps, but the years of training and patience will pay off. In the second half of your productive life you will hit "your" full stride, whatever that is. It may not be what you expected (it could be more or less), but it will be a vocation that is "optimum" for you. It will be a vocation or calling of substance. You will make a difference. It will matter that you have walked the face of the planet. You will do something with your life.

FOCUS QUESTIONS

1. Have you felt stuck in a career rut, and why or why not?
2. Referring to figure 1.1, how do your motivated abilities match up to your job description?
3. Answer the following questions as you reflect on your first half. Explain your answers.

   • Did you get what you wanted?
   • Has it made you happy?
   • Do you want to make a change?

4. In the first half of our productive adult lives we tend to focus on competence. During the second half we desire to do something of substance. Review the lists entitled "First Half" and "Second Half" on page 67. Where are you?
5. What is it that you want to do with your work life? How have you allowed God to shape your desires and calling? What can you do to make sure you hear God clearly for the second half of your career?

PART TWO

Finding Your Second Wind

SEVEN

Reconnecting with God—The Right Starting Point

*Most people have got just enough religion to
make them miserable.*

BILLY SUNDAY

ONE DAY MY SON ASKED IF I would pay to paint a basketball key and three-point line on our driveway. Since he had been so diligent to practice, I agreed.

I was mildly surprised when the company we hired sent three men for this relatively simple task. After showing them what we had in mind, John and I retreated inside the house. About twenty minutes later I glanced out the window. All three men were huddled under the basket, and they were not looking very productive.

Curious, I went outside and said, "What's up? Is there some kind of a problem?"

"No problem at all," said the crew chief.

"Then what are you doing? Why is it taking so long to get started?" I asked.

"Oh," he said, then showed me how they had hung a plumb line with a weighted bob from the end of the basketball hoop. He continued, "We are checking, cross-checking, and rechecking all of our measurements to make sure we have the right starting point. We've learned from experience that unless you have the right starting point, everything else will turn out wrong."

"Makes sense to me," I said and sheepishly slunk back into the house.

What a powerful message: Unless we have the right starting point, everything else will turn out wrong.

Let's be honest with each other. You and I have run enough races to have picked the wrong starting point on countless occasions. Thinking about finding a second wind as we enter the second half of our productive adult lives, could anything be more important than making sure we have the right starting point?

The right starting point is God. The one who has knit us together in our mother's womb, who knows when we stand or sit, who determines our times and the exact places where we should live—he is the place to begin.

THE PROBLEM

Every crisis is in some sense a crisis of faith. Consider these reflections from men at their midpoint:

- Rick said, "At thirty-eight I had it all. I opened the package I had worked on for all those years, and it was empty."
- Eddie, forty-five, said, "My thing is 'peace on earth, good will toward men.' My problem is that I don't have any peace for me."
- James, fifty-five, said, "I need organized religion. I need to get back in the fold. I need to get back to where I belong."
- Frank, fifty-two, said, "I always wanted to give thirty percent to Christ and run the other seventy percent myself. I ended up losing everything."
- Mitch, mid-forties, said, "I feel my time with God evaporating."

God talk runs high; God walk runs low. Why is that?

As a culture we speak highly of God, but often as an enfeebled grandfather, appreciated for what he did in times past. It's not that we don't think highly of God—we do. We just don't think of him as relevant.

One hundred years ago God was the starting point for men and women searching for the meaning of life. In the twentieth century the starting point has shifted from God to man. In our culture the "I" is the all-important, the starting point. People want to know, "What's in this for me?" Many churches now tend to focus on meeting "my needs" instead of drawing us humbly to worship God the sovereign Creator and ruler of all. But, as theologian Karl Barth pointed out, we cannot call "God" by shouting "man" in a loud voice.

Barth went on to say that our knowledge of God suffers a chronic lack of objectivity: "We do not know what we are talking about when we talk about God, but we still want to talk about him."[1] Because we have tended to seek the God, or gods, we want, we do not know the God who is.

The result is a God who looks "a little skinny." David Wells, in his book *God in the Wasteland*, says, "It is one of the defining marks of Our Time that God is now weightless. I do not mean by this that he is ethereal but rather that he has become unimportant."[2]

How did it get to be like this? In the African worldview the spiritual realm controls the physical. So when something goes badly the African asks, "*Why* did this happen?" The first thought always goes to the spiritual reason behind the physical event.

The Euro-American worldview, on the other hand, is more "horizontal" and man-centered. So when something goes wrong for us we ask, "*How* did this happen?" Our focus tends to be on fixing, controlling, manipulating. If we can understand how it happened (and can fix it), we often don't worry about why. That's because our view of man is so high.

This has led our culture to a small view of God. A small view of God has led to a small response, even among people of faith. This man-centered perspective of religion has "flattened out" faith. We are producing a generation of Christians who are orthodox in belief but secular in behavior. In other words, they have "right belief" but not "right practice." The Bible calls this disobedience.

Increasingly, however, more and more people want to reconnect to God. After thirty, forty, fifty, or more years of living "horizontally" they want to pay more attention to what's happening "vertically."[3]

OUR NEED FOR GOD

My wife, Patsy, recently observed, "People are going crazy over their cholesterol and spending billions of dollars and hours to extend their lives for five or ten years. But then each will die and go to heaven or hell. Why don't people spend more time worrying about that? Why don't we spend our time and money encouraging them to think about that?" Good questions.

In *The Fourth Turning*, authors William Strauss and Neil Howe suggest we sometimes perceive our civic challenge like an unsolvable Rubik's cube. Each time we identify a problem we see behind it another problem that must be solved first, and behind that problem another, and another, and so on.

For example, to fix crime we must fix the family, but first we have to fix welfare, but that means fixing the budget, but to do that we must fix our civic spirit, yet that won't happen until we fix our moral standards, and that means fixing our schools and churches, which means fixing our inner cities, and that's impossible unless we fix crime.

They suggest we have no "fulcrum" on which to rest a policy lever. "People of all ages sense that something huge will have to sweep across America before the gloom can be lifted—but that's an awareness we suppress. As a nation, we're in deep denial." [4]

I believe the "something huge" that must sweep across America is a wholesale return to God. But it must voluntarily sweep across America one person at a time.

After World War II the emperor of Japan said to General Douglas MacArthur, "I'll make Japan a Christian nation."

MacArthur thought about it for a day or two before he responded. "No, then Japan wouldn't be truly Christian. The people must come to Christ voluntarily." [5]

Midlife is a robust, hopeful season. What gives it such potential is the prospect of "something huge" sweeping across us, reinvigorating our spirits, wooing us to live the second half with the passion that can only come from being rightly connected to God. He is the right starting point, the plumb line, the fulcrum.

Like a huge rat halfway through the digestive system of a snake, roughly seventy-five million baby boomers form a huge demographic lump around the halfway mark of life. As we each respond to our own need to reconnect with God, perhaps our generation can return our nation to sanity.

In the turbulent hour of midlife, most of us will, or should, connect or reconnect with God in a real, deep, and meaningful way.

THREE WAYS TO BUILD

From a spiritual perspective we each build our lives one of three ways:

- Build on the wrong foundation.
- Build wrongly on the right foundation.
- Build rightly on the right foundation.

With which category do you most closely identify? Let's look more closely at each of these.

BUILD ON THE WRONG FOUNDATION

Danish philosopher and writer Søren Kierkegaard selected as his life's work the difficult task of teaching Christianity to people convinced they were already Christians. When Kierkegaard would ask his fellow Danes about how to live they all had the same answer: "We are Christians."

Yet he found these were people who often had never once entered a church, never thought about God, and never mentioned his name except in oaths. "Are all of them Christians who call themselves Christians?" He saw little resemblance between these comfortable middle-class people and the apostles and martyrs.[6]

Perhaps we have the same problem today. A *U.S. News and World Report* survey found eighty-eight percent of American adults are certain they are going to heaven. (Ironically, only sixty-seven percent are actually certain there is a heaven).[7] Are all of these who call themselves Christians, Christian?

Some of us have just enough religion to deceive ourselves into thinking we have all we need.

An accounting firm hired a young, green CPA and assigned him their fledgling H. W. Lay Company account. He lived frugally and regularly purchased small amounts of stock in the company. Later he joined them as controller. They made potato chips.

Rapid growth created a high pressure life, but the company we know as Frito-Lay prospered, and this man became quite wealthy. This led to a high visibility lifestyle for his wife and him. One observer said they lived "big," dividing their time between a Dallas penthouse and a cliff-side home in Hawaii.

Decades later, the owner of the accounting firm went to visit the CPA he had hired so many years earlier. As they sat in the panoramic living room of his expansive Hawaiian home he found an empty, angry man who cursed life and treated his wife with disrespect and rancor.

He had everything he wanted but nothing he needed.

Some of us picked the wrong starting point. We built on the wrong foundation. We embraced a philosophy that has proven vacant and hollow. It didn't deliver. And we, too, feel empty and angry.

One day a middle-aged man lost his job as the anchor for the local six o'clock news. Shattered, he turned to his female co-anchor who had quietly modeled God's love and care to him. In the darkest moment of his life he surrendered his life to God.

Later he said, "I never rejected God. I just never embraced him."

Have you embraced God? Or have you been building on the wrong foundation? The Bible says, "No one can lay any foundation other than the one already laid, which is Jesus Christ" (1 Corinthians 3:11).

Did you pick the right starting point? Jesus Christ is the plumb line, the right starting point, as the prophet Amos recorded.

"This is what he showed me: The Lord was standing by a wall that had been built true to plumb, with a plumb line in his hand. And the Lord asked me, 'What do you see, Amos?'

"'A plumb line,' I replied.

"Then the Lord said, 'Look, I am setting a plumb line among my people . . .'" (Amos 7:7–8).

How do people make it without God? The point is, they don't. C. S. Lewis once said that before you can make a person a Christian you must first convince him he is a pagan. If you have arrived at the middle of your life and realize you have not been building on the right foundation, the message of this book for you is, to quote Paul, "that [you] must turn to God in repentance and have faith in our Lord Jesus" (Acts 20:21).

If that's your heart's desire then you can lay the right foundation right now by giving your life to God in prayer. Pray from your depths, or you may use this suggested prayer.

Dear God, I have built on the wrong foundation. By faith I ask you to become my foundation, the starting point for the rest of my journey. I turn to You in repentance and put my faith in the Lord Jesus who died for my sins so that I might have eternal life. Amen.

If you have just trusted Christ to be your foundation, welcome to the family. In the days, weeks, and years ahead I know from my own experience and the experiences of others that you will look back on this as the most important decision you have ever made. Tell your spouse, your pastor, and close friends. The more you talk about it, the more it will help you conceptualize what you have done. Besides, many of these people will be ecstatic for you. Also, associate with a church community where Jesus Christ is the focal point.

BUILD WRONGLY ON THE RIGHT FOUNDATION

The Billy Graham Evangelistic Association reports that ninety percent of Christians lead defeated lives. Apparently, some ninety percent of professing Christians are not deeply committed and, as a result, do not consider themselves successful Christians. Just because we have the right foundation doesn't guarantee we will build in a right way.[8]

The Bible says we can build on our foundation two ways—rightly or wrongly. One way is building with gold, silver, and precious stones. The other way is building with wood, hay, and straw.

"If any man builds on this foundation using gold, silver, costly stones, wood, hay or straw, his work will be shown for what it is, because the Day will bring it to light. It will be revealed with fire, and the fire will test the quality of each man's work. If what he has built survives, he will receive his reward. If it is burned up, he will suffer loss; he himself will be saved, but only as one escaping through the flames" (1 Corinthians 3:12–15).

Notice the one who builds wrongly but on the right foundation will still be with God—"he himself will be saved." However, that person will suffer loss. How is it that people build with wood, hay, and straw?

Worldliness. We build wrongly when we become worldly. Worldliness is the harbinger of disaster for people of faith. To be worldly means to let the yeast of culture work its way through our lives. It is to "add" Jesus to our lives but not give up our idol. It is to invite Christ to be Savior but not Lord. It is to live by "cultural" rather than "biblical" ideas. It is to seek the God we want instead of the God who is. Worldliness means trying to be a kingdom person and a worldly person at the same time. It will drown you, as the following analogy illustrates.

Imagine for a moment that the world is made up completely of hydrogen, and the kingdom of God is made up completely of oxygen. You must have oxygen to live, so you must live in the kingdom. If you had only hydrogen you would perish, so you cannot live in the world.

Often, we try to have our cake and eat it too by living in the kingdom and in the world at the same time. But when we mix hydrogen and oxygen together we get water—H_2O. That means there is no longer oxygen. When we try to combine the world and the kingdom we will eventually suffocate. You can't breathe water. You will eventually drown.

By midlife we understand the correlation between cost and value. Dietrich Bonhoeffer expounds on the spiritual dimension of this in *The Cost of Discipleship*. He writes, "Cheap grace is the deadly enemy of our Church. When Christ calls a man he bids him come and die."

Bonhoeffer extols costly grace, a grace that must be sought again and again. It is costly because it calls us to follow Jesus Christ. We must take up our cross daily and follow him. It is costly because it cost God the life of his Son, and what has cost God much we cannot cheapen. We have been bought with a price.[8]

By the second half, every human being has paid a steep price to either build or not build on the foundation of Christ. We each have enough mileage on us to see that Christ is the "pearl of great value." It's time to make sure we build in a right way. In Chapter 18, "Walking with God—Cultivating a Hunger for the God Who Is," we will look at eight practical ideas to build on our foundation in a right way.

BUILD RIGHTLY ON THE RIGHT FOUNDATION

The Gallup Organization found that about ten percent of Americans are what they term "deeply committed" Christians. Another source concluded about eight percent are "religiously committed."

I think it's safe to assume that about ten percent of Americans have been building rightly on the right foundation. If you belong to this streamlined group, congratulations. I trust you will help pass it on.

Focus Questions

1. On a regular daily basis, what (or who) is your "starting point," your "foundation"?
2. In your life what competes with making God your starting point, and how?
3. Which of the three ways we build best describes how you have built your life, and why?

   • I have built on the wrong foundation.
   • I have built wrongly on the right foundation.
   • I have built rightly on the right foundation.

4. Which of the following best (and most honestly) describes how you have thought of God, and why?

   • God is "out there" but not that relevant to me.
   • I believe in God, but it's up to me to make what I will of my life.
   • God loves me, but I'm on my own.
   • He is the God who meets my needs.
   • He is the sovereign, holy, Creator God who "is."

5. How has this chapter challenged you to think differently about God? Are you at a point where you want to reconnect with God? How will you do it? In this chapter a prayer was suggested that you can use to connect, or reconnect, with God. Here it is again if you would like to sincerely invite Christ to be your Savior and Lord.

Dear God, I have built on the wrong foundation. By faith I ask you to become my foundation, the starting point for the rest of my journey. I turn to You in repentance and put my faith in the Lord Jesus who died for my sins so that I might have eternal life. Amen.

E I G H T

Habitual Thinking—Defeating This Ally of Mediocrity

*Genius . . . means little more than the faculty of perceiving
in an unhabitual way.*

WILLIAM JAMES

DURING THE EIGHTEENTH CENTURY, ARCHITECTS MASTER-PLANNED the entire city of St. Petersburg, Russia, before the first shovel of dirt was turned. Today you can walk freely along the streets of St. Petersburg, a city unrivaled in forethought and beauty.

To accommodate the master plan, numerous large rocks had to be removed. As fate would have it, one particularly large boulder was deposited right in the middle of a major avenue. The city administrators solicited bids for its removal. Because labor-saving modern equipment and explosives didn't exist, the bids came in high—too high.

As the officials wondered what to do, a peasant presented himself and offered to get rid of the boulder for a much lower price than the other bidders. Having nothing to lose they gave him the job.

The next day the peasant showed up with a small army of other peasants carrying shovels. Right next to the rock they dug a huge hole deeper than the rock was high. Next they pushed the rock into the hole so that no part of the rock was street level. Then they filled in dirt around the edges and carted off the remaining dirt in wheelbarrows.

By thinking in a nonhabitual way, this enterprising peasant was able to solve a problem that no one else could figure out.

THE PROBLEM

Webster's defines mediocrity to mean "barely adequate, inferior, poor to moderate in quality."

The greatest ally of mediocrity is habitual thinking. It is not our critical, creative, or careful thinking that spawns mediocrity; it is our habitual thinking.

Habitual means "established by long use." In *A Brief History of Time*, physicist Stephen Hawking describes what may be the all time classic illustration of habitual thinking. Aristotle had said that a heavy body would fall faster than a light one because it would have a greater pull toward the earth. He worked this theory out through reason. Apparently, not until Galileo, some 1900 years later, did anyone actually check the theory through observation.[1]

In an apocryphal story, Galileo climbed to the top of the leaning tower of Pisa and dropped two objects of different weights. The objects landed at precisely the same instant. So vested were the observers in the old theory that they refused to believe what they had seen.

By midlife we have all acquired a long list of habits, some good and some not so good, that help us organize our lives. Some of these routines make life convenient, like grooming rituals and customs for coexisting with a mate. Actually, most habits bless us. They save time—think how easy it is to open a computer file today versus when you were just learning. They also relieve pressure—think how much more attention you must pay to driving in another city versus your own familiar streets.

Some habits, though, keep us from reaching our full potential. They protrude and create unwanted drag, like a plane trying to take off with the flaps down. Occasionally they can even keep us from getting off the ground at all. We've all heard the cliché about the man who, though he worked for his company thirty years, had one year of experience thirty times.

The purpose of this chapter is to get you thinking. In his book *A Whack on the Side of the Head*, Roger von Oech says nothing is more dangerous than an idea when it's the only one you have. He suggests we look for the second right idea, adding "The best way to get a good idea is to get a lot of ideas."[2]

In this chapter I would like to present a lot of ideas about habitual thinking that I hope will jar open your own thinking. Let's see if we can ferret out the habitual thinking that has slowed us down, cast us into the lake, and brought us to the brink of mediocrity. Let's go on a "habit hunt" together.

EXAMPLES OF HABITUAL THINKING

Some habitual thinking is just funny, some of it is destructive, and some of it is just plain dumb. Here are a few examples from "funny/dumb."

I keep a bottle of Advil in my glove compartment because the glare from driving sometimes gives me a headache. Recently I leaned across the front seat while speeding down the expressway to reach for my bottle. Since I keep it on the right-hand side of the glove box, I always swerve a little as I reach.

All of a sudden it dawned on me. For the seven years I've owned this car, the Advil bottle has always been in the exact same place. It occurred to me, however, that if I moved it to the left-hand side of the glove box I wouldn't have to lean all the way across the seat to get at the bottle. It would be a full twelve inches closer (I measured for this book), which would make a much safer situation. Habitual thinking.

Every first and third Monday morning the leadership team from the men's Bible study I teach meets at my home office. Every time we meet I make coffee for the men. And every time we meet I do the same thing. I go into our kitchen (about a hundred feet away), get our coffee container, walk back to my office, measure out the coffee into the coffee maker, walk back into our kitchen to return the coffee, then turn around and go back out to the office for the meeting. That's a football field plus a hundred feet of walking.

Not long ago it struck me: *Why don't you get a separate can of coffee just for your meetings?* Duh. I estimated that I had made that twice-monthly trip nearly three hundred times—walking about twenty-three miles—before it dawned on me how simple it would be to keep a second container of coffee! Habitual thinking.

What are your "boy, was that dumb" habits?

Some habitual thinking will simply drive you nuts. For twenty-five years I have asked Patsy, "Please write the purpose of the check on the stub." The other day we were trying to figure out our IRS payments. None of the stubs were marked, so I couldn't tell exactly what was going on. I said, "Patsy! Why can't you write that tiny piece of information on these stubs! I don't get it!" Things were a bit chilly until I apologized.

Some habitual thinking can get serious. We live near the end of a dead-end street. One day we noticed a dog hanging around our yard. This went on for a couple of days until we realized that the dog lived somewhere beyond the end of our dead-end street. But because he was blocked he didn't know what to do. My wife drove the neighborhoods looking for lost-dog signs. The dog was starving so she fed him (of course it was a "him") for over a week. Eventually the animal shelter had to come pick him up.

Some habitual thinking leads to poor decision making. It's been said that those who do not know history are doomed to repeat it. Peter Berger, the sociologist, has said there are cycles to history. Time is cyclical, not just linear. He says we need to wake up; there's more going on than we think. In their groundbreaking books, *Generations* and *The Fourth Turning*, William Strauss and Neil Howe reveal the implications of habitual thinking at a societal and cultural level. One point they make is that we have been dramatically shaped by the cultural and historical forces at work in our generation. These forces create habitual thinking.

How has habitual thinking led you to make some poor decisions?

LYING, CHEATING, AND STEALING

By the end of the first half of our productive adult lives, some of us have been in the river too long. We've let bad habits waterlog our brain tissue.

Bob changed companies recently, but stayed in the wholesale plant business. During his employment interview he told his employer, "I will never lie for you or to you. My reasoning is that if I lied for you, you would never know for sure if I was lying to you." His new employer seemed impressed.

Not long after Bob went to work, he was placed in charge of a large account. He had heard scuttlebutt about a "special" arrangement on this customer's billings. His boss pulled him aside and explained that this customer did not count its own inventory, but relied on the company to track how many plants were being sold.

"Once," he said, "we accidentally billed the customer twice for the same plants, but by the time we discovered the error we had already spent the money on some new equipment. So, from time to time since then, when we have needed a new piece of equipment, we just send them an extra bill. Bob, we have such a need now, and I want you to make up the invoice."

Bob was rocked, but kept his composure. He said, "Do you remember what I said in my initial interview? I said I would never lie for you or to you. What you are asking me to do is wrong, and I can't do it. Beyond that, I don't believe God can bless your business if you are going to use these kinds of practices."

It was his boss's turn to be rocked. He said, "You know, Bob, you are completely right. This is wrong. I just can't understand how I could have been so blind. What's wrong with me, anyway? You know, I grew up in the church. I wasn't brought up this way. I've been a fool."

Do you have any habitual thinking that has led to an integrity problem? Think it over. Should you make some midpoint adjustments in this area? It might be as complex as the story just told, or as simple as not converting company office supplies to personal use.

DRAWING OUTSIDE THE LINES

Remember this? Everyone has seen the "nine dots" riddle, but you probably haven't seen it in a while.

The task is to connect all nine dots by making four straight lines and you are not allowed to lift your pencil from the paper or retrace a line. If you don't remember how to do it, give it a try before going further or check the solution at the end of the chapter.

The point of the riddle is that habitual thinking leads us to try solving the riddle by drawing inside the lines. To break out of habitual thinking we have to learn how to think "outside the lines."

EXAMPLES OF "OUTSIDE THE LINES" THINKING

Standing on top of Coit Tower in San Francisco you can gaze back across the city. As you pan the grid of interlocking streets, a funny looking zigzag grabs your attention. The eight curves of Lombard Street make it the world's most famous street. Funny. Nobody knows the names of the streets on either side. Lombard Street is a metaphor for "outside the lines" thinking.

In Carmel, California, The Pebble Beach Company has created one of the all-time classic examples of thinking "outside the lines." Out of thin air they have created and packaged the famous "17-Mile Drive." For about five dollars you can drive through their development and look at a single tree, a lone rock, a swirl in the ocean, and a few other benign sights (trust me).

The day we drove through you literally could not find a place to park to look at what the brochure proclaimed as "the lone pine tree." There were over fifty cars, some trying to park in people's yards. Competitive juices flowed as men jockeyed their cars for position so their families could look at this tree standing all by itself. I'm not making this up.

My favorite story of overcoming habitual thinking has always been Roger Bannister.

Running the mile in less than four minutes had been deemed an impossible feat—a physical impossibility, an unpassable barrier. Many tried; no one could do it. They said it couldn't be done (could we be "they"?). A less-than-four-minute mile was impossible. Except they forgot to tell that to Roger Bannister.

On May 6, 1954 in Oxford, England, Roger Bannister rounded the last bend on a record-shattering pace. To the utter astonishment of habitual thinkers everywhere, as he broke the tape the clock flashed a time of 3 minutes 59.4 seconds. By "outside the lines" thinking Roger Bannister, knighted for his achievement, became the first human being to ever run a mile in less than four minutes. But even that's not what is most interesting.

What's really interesting is that a mere month later John Landy also ran a mile in less than four minutes and broke Bannister's record. Over the next year, a dozen men also ran the mile in less than four minutes. Once the barrier of "habitual thinking" had been broken, people realized it had been a psychological rather than a physical barrier.

Thank God for the Roger Bannisters of the world—men and women who elevate themselves and, in so doing, inspire whole generations to overcome the obstacles of habitual thinking through faith and hard work.

My second favorite story of overcoming habitual thinking pertains to Michael Jordan. When Michael Jordan elevates into outer space somewhere around the free throw line, soars through the air, and slam dunks the basketball through the hoop, our own spirits somehow soar with him. When he elevates himself, he somehow elevates us with him. We think higher than we did before. We think "Maybe." We think "Why not?"

As a boy Michael Jordan was cut from his high school basketball team because he wasn't good enough—not once, but twice! He had taken on the habitual thinking of some of the kids around him. Then he decided to live "outside the lines" and do something with his life. Radical thinking.

What can you do to live "outside the lines" during the second half?

FOCUS QUESTIONS

1. Can you give an example of how habitual thinking has been helpful for you? How about an example that has kept you from reaching your full potential?
2. What do you celebrate in other people? In what ways has habitual thinking caused you to be negative? Positive?

3. Have you been told there is something that you simply cannot do? That it's impossible? Is that really true? Why or why not?

4. Discovering our habitual thinking will take some focused effort. Abandoning well-worn, comfortable habits is easier said than done. To think "outside the lines" will require a plan. A simple plan. I have here listed a number of bad habits of thought and action. As you scan the list, write down those that strike you as habits you need to eliminate from your life. Perhaps a trusted friend could review the list with you. Next to each item on your list, write down one or two ways you could think "outside the lines" about that habit.

worry	touchy feelings	white lies
lying	petty thievery	cheating
stealing	complaining	whining
critical spirit	judgmental	selfish ambitions
wrong motives	impure thoughts	grumbling
negative attitude		

Nine dots solution:

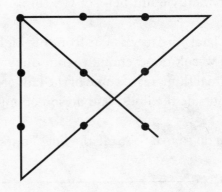

NINE

Overcoming Bitterness—Seeking Forgiveness and Forgiving

Forgiveness is the fragrance the violet leaves on the heel that crushed it.

MARK TWAIN

FOUR BROTHERS STRONGLY DISAGREED ABOUT THE type of health care needed for their aging mother. Two brothers ganged up against a third. The acrimony devastated the fourth.

After their mother died, the four brothers divided into two camps that don't speak to each other. That was eight years ago. Recently one brother's wife died from cancer. One of the other brothers not speaking to him finally picked up the phone many months after the funeral to express his sorrow and sympathy.

A mutual friend, upon hearing this, asked the brother who placed the call, "Does this mean that all is forgiven and you have reconciled?"

"No, not at all," came the response.

THE PROBLEM

We all have disappointments large and small that get us down. It may be a child making all the wrong choices and you don't know what to do. Maybe your spouse doesn't like you very much right now. Perhaps your child died, a grief my own parents have had to endure. For my parents, it's a grief never gotten over.

Maybe you have a great business idea, but you can't get anyone to back you. Perhaps financial success eludes you after all these years of trying to make it. You don't feel like you are respected. You have been passed over. Your body tells you that you're not getting any younger.

You have a chronic health problem. Your mate has a chronic health problem.

Possibly your disappointments are more daily. Your son would rather play basketball with another adult than you. Your wife doesn't express appreciation when you help around the house. Your neighbor keeps that huge camper parked next to your bedroom window.

Everyone has disappointments, but sometimes they smolder into bitterness. What is bitterness? Basically, bitterness is disappointment that hangs around. It is that unmistakable look on someone's face when you ask, "How are things going?" It is eyes that say, "Life has not been fair to me." It is a poison to the soul.

Bitterness is brooding over not getting what we want—especially when we think we are right and "they" are wrong. It is the feeling that won't go away when you are passed over for promotion, and you're convinced you would have been a better choice.

Bitterness is the spark of fury that lights when an old foe's name is mentioned. It is anger against God, not admitted even to one's self. Bitterness is the face of the one who wronged you that flashes when you awaken in the middle of the night. Bitterness is the price of not forgiving.

Bitterness occupies a closet in everyone's life. By the middle years we each accumulate an assortment of grievances, real and perceived, that can become large roadblocks to joy and peace in the second half. Part of reinventing ourselves for the second half is making peace with old disappointments. Easier said than done.

When Ed turned fifty he confided, "I've been bitter all my life. I have never acknowledged that what's happened to me could be God's will for my life. I have never accepted anything negative. I can never get past my disappointments. I could give you thirty examples."

This chapter outlines a plan to graduate from God's school. Perhaps the most important part of overcoming bitterness is to stop pretending we are not bitter. In an earlier chapter we ask, "How can a man get exactly what he wants and still not be happy?" In this chapter we ask, "How can a man not get what he wants and still be happy?"

The Bible reminds us: "Each heart knows its own bitterness, and no one else can share its joy" (Proverbs 14:10). Bitterness, like joy, is one of the deepest secrets of the heart. What is the thing that's eating away at you? What is your long-term problem that won't go away? That's what I would like us to focus on in this chapter.

PASSED OVER

One day I received a call from Promise Keepers, the Christian men's organization, to see if I would be interested in speaking at a local "wake up call" for men.

Since I work with men as a vocation, I had secretly hoped and prayed for just such an invitation for some time. Also, I assumed the "local" speaking assignment would be a type of "beauty contest" or audition. I guessed that if I did a good job they would probably offer a larger assignment.

The day came, and by God's grace I did an excellent job. About one third of the three thousand men attending responded to an invitation to make a deeper commitment to God. At the end I received a standing ovation.

Sure enough, a couple of months later I was invited to speak on a "national" conference program in Atlanta. I was so grateful. Once again I surmised that if I fulfilled my assignment, the possibility existed for an invitation to speak before one of their stadium events which often exceeded attendance of fifty thousand men. I hoped for such an assignment because I sincerely believe God has given me a message for men.

At the national conference I was asked to give two messages—a workshop on racial reconciliation and the closing keynote message for the conference. For weeks, as thoughts occurred to me, I wrote them on scraps of paper and stuck them in a file folder. All together I'm sure I spent over fifty hours preparing the two messages.

On a Wednesday afternoon I conducted the session on racial reconciliation. I knew from the beginning that it was going well. I had paid a high personal price for some of the ideas and illustrations, and I could tell from the men's faces that the fresh perspectives were truly helping.

I was scheduled to address the closing session the following night. Unfortunately, I was as unsure of the second message as I was sure of the first. On Thursday morning, I began making final preparations. It was coming ever so slowly. Some men working behind the scenes at the conference had agreed to pray that God would give me a message. Suddenly the thought came to title the message, "What Does It Mean to Love God with All Your Heart, Soul, Mind, and Strength?" *That's it!* I thought.

Joy flooded my soul as a deluge of ideas poured into my mind. At one point the idea came to ask the men, "What would it mean to love God with our eyes? ... our ears? ... our lips? ... our hands? ... our feet? ... our knees?" Then the answers started to form, "To love God with our eyes would mean that they would be often closed in prayer, that they would not wink at injustice, that they would not yield to the temptation to lust."

At one point the ideas came so fast and with such intensity that I began to weep and asked God to stay his hand. Throughout the day I put the finishing touches on the outline and memorized it.

As the time drew near I felt excitement coursing in my veins. I sensed I had "a message from God" for these men. I stood and spoke.

It was the worst nightmare of my life. I was too long. I was too preachy. It was horrible. After the message not one Promise Keeper official greeted me. A man from the audience came up and questioned something I said. I bit his head off. The next morning I caught a plane back home, depressed.

I knew there was no way I would ever be invited to speak at one of the large events they conduct in football stadiums. I had blown it, and it was devastating. To add salt to the wound, two weeks later I gave the same message (although shorter) in the same city to a different audience and had one of a handful of the greatest responses ever.

To be very honest with you, I must confess that I struggled for a long time with anger toward God. I truly believed, and still believe, that God gave me that message. That two weeks later God blessed the message as much as I had blown it earlier only made it worse. I had wanted something, and now it was never going to happen. The disappointment clobbered me.

A seed of bitterness toward God kept putting out feeler roots, trying to find fertile soil. Eventually I made my peace with God. I simply had to trust that he had something else he wanted me to do, some other direction he wanted me to go. I had to have faith that he knows what's best for me better than I know for myself. With that, I put it behind me and moved on.

Over a year came and went. One morning I awakened early and went into my study. I was having a remarkable time of Bible reading, prayer, and meditation. After nearly an hour and a half the memory of being passed over as a Promise Keeper speaker came to mind. Suddenly, I was right back in the middle of it. A fifteen-foot-high storm surge of bitterness swept over me. *Where in the world did that come from?* I wondered.

I sat there stunned not only by the recurrence of this bitterness, but by its intensity. I then said three things to myself . . .

1. That's not spiritual.
2. I won't allow that.
3. I'm not bitter.

Guess what that accomplished? Not a thing. These three statements were little more than "self-talk" and positive-thinking gibberish.

At the end of the first half, most of us have something major that didn't turn out the way we hoped. Often, the result is bitterness. Our joy in the second half may well depend on what we do about that.

STEPS TO OVERCOMING BITTERNESS

How can we put bitterness behind us? The first step in overcoming bitterness is to stop pretending you are not bitter. "In bitterness of soul Hannah wept much and prayed." Jeremiah said, "He has besieged me and surrounded me with bitterness and hardship." Ezekiel said, "The Spirit then lifted me up and took me away, and I went in bitterness and in the anger of my spirit." Job said, "I loathe my very life; therefore I will give free rein to my complaint and speak out in the bitterness of my soul." So many of the great heroes of the Bible felt bitterness.

The presence of bitterness alone is not a sin. Yet, bitterness left to fester can become sin. The Bible says, "Get rid of all bitterness, rage and anger" (Ephesians 4:31). So if you are bitter, don't pretend you are not.

The second step in overcoming bitterness is to allow the grace, or kindness, of God to work in your heart. The Bible says, "It does not, therefore, depend on man's desire or effort, but on God's mercy" (Romans 9:16). This gives us three possible ways to live:

- man's desire
- man's effort
- God's mercy

The point is that we cannot "will" ourselves out of bitterness (our desire); we cannot "work" ourselves out of bitterness (our effort); we must seek God's "grace" to deliver us from bitterness (his mercy).

In my case, I had to admit that saying, "That's not spiritual," didn't line up with biblical examples. I also had to admit that saying, "I won't allow that," was little more than depending on my own "desire" and "effort." Finally, I had to admit that it was not honest to say, "I am not bitter," because I was.

What does the grace of God enable us to do? Grace gives us the strength to offer, seek, and receive forgiveness.

OFFER FORGIVENESS

For years I have followed trials in which a child or young adult was tragically killed or severely injured. What fascinates me most is how differently the parents respond.

On one occasion the parents seethe with unquenchable rage. When the verdict is announced we sense no satisfaction for them. Our internal "voice analyzer" tells us that these people are bitter, unhappy, and miserable.

On another occasion we observe parents who, while sad, have found peace. What's the difference? Philip Chandler, a young teenager in Orlando, was stuffed in a hot trunk and left for dead by two delinquents. When he was finally found he was foaming at the mouth. Because of brain damage he will never live a normal life. Yet, Philip's parents found it in their hearts to offer forgiveness to the two boys who did this heinous act. That doesn't mean they want to see the boys go free. They still want the boys held accountable for their actions. Yet, by forgiving the sin they set themselves free from the stranglehold of bitterness.

Jesus said, "For if you forgive men when they sin against you, your heavenly Father will also forgive you. But if you do not forgive men their sins, your Father will not forgive your sins" (Matthew 6:14–15).

REPEATEDLY OFFER FORGIVENESS

When seat belts were first introduced in the 1960s, do you remember the slogan drilled into our heads? "Most accidents take place within twenty-five miles of home." What they didn't mention is, of course, the reason why: Most driving takes place within twenty-five miles of home.

We could also say that most slights, insults, grudges, grievances, offenses, indignities, and bitternesses take place within twenty-five miles of home. Most of our bitternesses will develop against people with whom we have regular contact—husbands, wives, children, in-laws, parents, coworkers, bosses, customers.

The repetitive nature of sins like cutting remarks or a controlling personality can lead quickly to bitterness. Perhaps the apostle Peter was thinking of someone like that when he asked Jesus, "Lord, how many times shall I forgive my brother when he sins against me? Up to seven times?"

Jesus answered, "I tell you, not seven times, but seventy-seven times" (Matthew 18:21–22). Speaking in hyperbole, Jesus meant as often as someone sins against you—to protect you from bitterness of heart—forgive them. Notice that Jesus says forgive without regard to whether or not the party who offended you seeks forgiveness! Forgiving others is not contingent on their seeking forgiveness. Forgiving them is for the health of your heart—not theirs. If they seek forgiveness then they can get a healthy heart too. But don't let what they do—or don't do—block you from setting yourself free from the gnarly, tangled root of bitterness.

Again, Jesus says, "When you stand praying, if you hold anything against anyone, forgive him, so that your Father in heaven may forgive you your sins" (Mark 11:25).

This is a most remarkable claim and promise. But how can you possibly forgive someone who isn't sorry? The answer is that we forgive them by faith. We don't excuse their offense. We don't say we must trust them. But we do say, "As far as it is up to me, by faith I forgive this person's sin against me."

A woman's husband divorced her, and he turned out to be a real jerk during the process. He planned the divorce well in advance and stiffed her financially. Yet, rather than getting on with her life, many years later her bitterness toward him controls her speech, her countenance, her thoughts, her life. If she could only forgive him by faith. Then she could get on with reinventing herself for the rest of the journey.

SEEK FORGIVENESS

We all surely know that in the same way we have been hurt by others, we have hurt them. Perhaps for years you have had a critical spirit, a nagging way, or an unappreciative attitude toward your spouse.

Prune out all the branches of bitterness by seeking forgiveness— even if seventy times seven times. Jesus put it this way: "Therefore, if you are offering your gift at the altar and there remember that your brother has something against you, leave your gift there in front of the altar. First go and be reconciled to your brother; then come and offer your gift" (Matthew 5:23–24).

In short, Jesus means that "reconciliation precedes worship." That's a powerful statement for our behavior.

PUT DOWN YOUR LOAD

Have you been completely honest with yourself about your bitternesses? Often we think we must carry the burden of the past.

Hannah Whitall Smith told the story about an old hunched over man walking down a dusty road with a heavy backpack across his shoulders. A fellow traveler in a wagon pulled up and invited him aboard. A few minutes down the road the wagoneer glanced over and was surprised to see the old man had not taken off the heavy pack.

"Old fellow, when I offered you a ride I meant to take a load off you. Take off that pack, now, and put it down in the wagon."

"Oh no, young man, I couldn't do that. It was enough that you offered me this ride. I couldn't expect you to carry my burden, too."[1]

Like a heavy burden across our shoulders, many of us feel we must continue to bear the bitterness of our soul. God wants to say something to you: "Take off that pack, now, and put it down in the wagon."

FOCUS QUESTIONS

1. "Perhaps the most important part of overcoming bitterness is to quit pretending we are not bitter." Do you agree or not, and why?
2. What feelings of bitterness do you still hold? Why is it such a struggle to let go?
3. What do you think will happen to you in the second half if you fail to overcome your bitterness?
4. Who are the people who have repeatedly hurt you that you struggle to forgive? To what degree will your happiness or bitterness over the next five years depend on whether or not you forgive these people? If this applies to you, by faith pledge yourself to forgive these people their sins against you.
5. Who are the people you suspect you have wronged who may have bitternesses built up against you (think "within twenty-five miles of home")? Why not pledge yourself to go to these people, apologize, and ask their forgiveness? If you find that idea difficult, why do you think you resist it? If going to them physically is not practical or wise, seek God's forgiveness and let it go.

TEN

Managing Expectations—The Key to Overcoming Disappointment

All disappointment is the result of unmet expectations.

AT THE AGES OF FIFTY-TWO AND fifty-one, two friends who work together have accumulated as much knowledge, experience, wisdom, and credibility as any two people in their field. During their careers they have developed some progressive ideas that could revolutionize their industry.

Over three years they developed a carefully considered, reasonable business plan. This plan captures their idea on paper the way Monet captures wildflowers on canvas. Both men burn with passion to make the rest of their adult productive lives count. Yet, in over two years they have not found any willing backers. It has been very frustrating.

THE PROBLEM

For every twenty-three hundred high school senior basketball players, forty will become college players, and only one will make it onto an NBA roster.

Every youngster who ever played a team sport has dreamed of playing in the big leagues. Most of those youngsters never make it to the varsity squad of their high school team. Of those who do, the closest they will ever get to the majors is a seat behind left center field.

Early in life we know where we stand in the athletic pecking order of life. While I was deeply disappointed to be the final boy cut from my seventh grade basketball team, at least I knew where I stood.

In other areas of life it takes a good deal longer to figure out where you stand. By midlife, though, the rest of the picture comes into focus.

Within limits, you know whether or not you're going to make a million dollars. You know whether or not you're going to be in top management. You know whether or not people will seek you out for your counsel.

You know whether or not your children will make you proud of them. You know whether or not you are happily married. You know whether or not you have found a purpose big enough to last a lifetime. You know whether or not success the way you defined it has satisfied you.

Much of our dissatisfaction with life comes from unmet expectations—expectations that seemed realistic but, in hindsight, probably were not.

All disappointment is the result of unmet expectations. In other words, we don't experience disappointment about things we never expected in the first place. Rather, we experience disappointment when a dream, desire, or plan goes up in smoke.

The key, then, to overcoming disappointment is to effectively manage our expectations.

Managing Expectations

At the age of forty-five, Ted, married twenty-six years with sons ages twenty and seventeen, watched his career of twelve years evaporate. Like a prospector panning for gold, he has spent the last year searching every corner of his community for a fresh career path. Nothing has worked out yet.

"This is by far the biggest challenge we have ever had to face," he began. "Yet, we have been through many other gains and losses. I guess you might say we are 'struggle hardened.' I suppose I see life as a mixture of ups and downs, victories and defeats, mountains and valleys, some sweet and some filled with sorrow.

"Frankly, I don't usually ask the 'why' questions—I'm just not wired that way. I have always felt that if I took a just position, in the end I would prevail. It doesn't always happen, does it? Justice may not come through. Things may not turn out like we want. I think I put way too much confidence in systems and appeal processes. I've been humbled. Yet, this has brought me to trust God more.

"This has also brought our family closer—we'll get through this. What keeps me going is to know this is a blip in eternity. Sometimes I think about giving up, but so far it's just a fleeting thought."

This man has figured out how to manage his expectations. He has learned to be happy even when his "Plan A" has been difficult. What should be our reasonable expectations when we reach the midpoint of our adult life?

Our expectations should be a balance of joy and suffering. Let's look what our expectations should be from several perspectives.

THIS IS PLAN A

A fifty-two-year-old woman endured a terrible marriage that ended abruptly when her husband of twenty-eight years announced on Christmas Day that he was divorcing her. About a year later she heard a seminar speaker say that whatever we are going through is "Plan A." It was a difficult thought for her to accept at first, then liberating.

The purpose of theology is to examine all that can be gleaned about a subject in Scripture, then to form a "position" or doctrine that summarizes what the Bible teaches. One such idea that brings immense comfort in sorrows is the sovereignty of God.

Every day millions of people throughout the world pray in the Lord's Prayer: "Your kingdom come, Your will be done, on earth as it is in heaven." There are only two possibilities. First, God hears these prayers and because he is all-good and all-powerful his "Plan A" is being done. The second option is that his will is not being done, the world operates under "Plan B," and God is not the sovereign Lord of creation.

But how can my situation be Plan A? you wonder. How can we explain the frustration, futility, and meaningless that hold so much of the world in its grasp?

If stranded on a desert island and told I could tear only one page out of my Bible to keep, I would pick the page that contains Romans 8. If later told I could keep only one paragraph, it would be verses 18 through 21:

> I consider that our present sufferings are not worth comparing with the glory that will be revealed in us. The creation waits in eager expectation for the sons of God to be revealed.

For the creation was subjected to frustration, not by its own choice, but by the will of the one who subjected it, in hope that the creation itself will be liberated from its bondage to decay and brought into the glorious freedom of the children of God.

Notice first that "our present sufferings" are a given. This passage, written to Christians, assumes suffering. Jesus said, "In this world you will have trouble" (John 16:33). That's because "the creation was subjected to frustration."

You and I, as part of "the creation," are subject to "frustration." Frustration means that overwhelming sense of futility, meaninglessness, or lack of purpose that sweeps over people from time to time. Frustration is different than evil. While evil is that which is wicked, frustration is simply that which is pointless. It's what makes us cry out, "What's the point? What's it all about? Is this all there is?"

Solomon fully captured the "pointless" feeling when he said, "Meaningless! Meaningless! . . . Utterly meaningless! Everything is meaningless!" (Ecclesiastes 1:2). It is fascinating that in the Septuagint (the third-century B.C. Greek translation of the Old Testament) the translators chose to translate Solomon's "meaninglessness" into Greek with the same word used for "frustration" in Romans 8. In others words, Solomon's "meaninglessness" is the same thing as Paul's "frustration"!

There is another notable difference between frustration and evil. Notice where this frustration comes from: "Not by its own choice, but by the will of the one [God] who subjected it." In other words, God doesn't just allow frustration and futility, he causes it.

But why would he do that? No one can fully understand why God would allow evil. We can understand, however, why God would cause frustration. Frustration is a gracious gesture of God to deliver us. When we feel the full weight of how futile the world is, we cry out to God for deliverance. In other words, the "thorns and thistles" of the Fall become the pricks by which we abandon our self-will and turn to God. God "pricks" us "in hope that the creation itself [us] will be liberated from its bondage to decay and brought into the glorious freedom of the children of God."

God is sovereignly orchestrating all things according to the purpose of his will. Nothing happens apart from the will of God. Two sparrows are bought and sold for a few inflated pennies, yet not one of them falls to the ground apart from the will of God (see Matthew 10:29).

God does answer our prayer, his will is being done, and he is Lord. Everything that happens to us happens for a purpose. Our pain is real, but the purpose is good. "I consider that our present sufferings are not worth comparing with the glory that will be revealed in us." This is Plan A.

EXPECT THORNS AND THISTLES

When eagles build their nests they begin with branches as thick as four inches and as long as eight feet. To this they add smaller branches, and eventually leaves and perhaps an animal skin.

When her eggs are about to hatch, mother eagle pulls downy fur from her breast and prepares a soft, warm bedding for the eaglets. Father eagle will gather a few toys—an old golf ball, a shoe, a tin can.

After the eaglets hatch, both parents hunt from sunup to sundown to feed the voracious appetites of their babies. As the weeks go by the eaglets enjoy a life of leisure. Eaglehood, however, isn't achieved by lounging comfortably in a feathered nest. Mother and father know the eaglets will soon have to provide food for themselves. So they enroll their children in Eagle School.

One lovely spring day the eaglets watch their mother glide into the nest, but they note a wild look in her eye. She squawks and stomps around the nest, picking up toys and hurling them over the side. The horrified children try to stay out of her way. Next mom grabs the rabbit fur blanket and slings it over the side. Golf ball, too. Then, with her great wings, she sweeps the nest clean of the downy featherbed. By the time she's done only the sticks and twigs remain.

The nest becomes a nuisance as the sticks poke into the baby eagles. All of a sudden they must use their talons to balance themselves. Finally, mom leaves to hunt for food. At first, they wobble back and forth on their precarious perch of twigs. Each passing day, however, their talons grow stronger, which will help later when they must carry a wriggling fish to their nest. The little eagles don't appreciate the value of these lessons. They only know it is difficult.[1]

So it is with us. There are thorns and thistles in life, and God put them there for our benefit because he loves us. God lowers us onto the branches so we may become strong. All we know is that it is difficult.

Life began in a garden, a garden so perfect we call it paradise. When Adam fell, however, God banished all humankind from this perfect place.

What's more, the ground to which we've been sent is cursed. We eat through painful toil and sweaty brow. We must do our work while feeling the prick of thorns.

Ironically, many people organize their entire lives around the goal of getting back into the garden—to build a comfortable, insulated life in a gated community. The tendency is to think, "If I could just get back into the garden everything would be all right." In this life it will never happen. As they say, you can't unscramble an egg. You can't rewrite history. We can't go back.

We don't live in a garden anymore. The world is no picnic. It's a briar patch, a rocky field, a concrete jungle.

What should be our reasonable expectation of the world? Our lives will be considerably more content if we expect the world that "is" and not the one we "want."

Babies whine and cry until they realize they can't get what they want. In fact, we know that if we give our babies everything they want we will spoil them. Yet, once they get over the temper tantrum, babies become quite content with life the way it is. So it is with us.

Have you accepted the world that way it "is"? As you float in the middle of the midlife lake, recalibrate your expectations to a "reasonable" level.

The Pruning Season

When you hit the wall the world will say, "You must be doing something wrong." Maybe. Maybe not. The assumption is that if you do "these things" then you will get what you want. If you do it "right" you can prevent troubles from coming. The Bible says differently.

The Bible says that, "[God] cuts off every branch in me that bears no fruit, while every branch that does bear fruit he prunes so that it will be even more fruitful."[2]

Let's think about this. If you are not fruitful you get cut off, but if you are fruitful you get trimmed clean. In other words, whether you produce fruit or not, you're going to get cut! (Nobody tells you this when you sign up!)

Any shrub or vine that isn't pruned gets leggy. Yet, the more you trim it the bushier it gets. Fruit only forms where branches are supple and flexible. Once a branch gets hard and woody it loses its shape and beauty. Its usefulness depends on the process of pruning.

Can you see your troubles as a pruning season? If so, entrust yourself to God. A painful wound is often inflicted for a kind purpose, like a surgeon's scalpel. You will be even more fruitful in the second half of your life.

FOCUS QUESTIONS

1. What is your greatest disappointment at the middle of life, and why?
2. Have your expectations tended to be realistic or not, and why? How have your expectations affected your attitude and general outlook on life?
3. What should be your reasonable expectations for:

   - Your relationship with your wife?
   - Your relationships with your children?
   - Your career?
   - Your health?
   - Your finances?
   - Your walk with God?

4. Have you considered that what has happened to you is part of God's "Plan A" for your life? Does the explanation of "frustration" in Romans 8:18–21 under the subheading This Is Plan A satisfy you, and why or why not? Give a personal example.

5. Three ideas were presented in this chapter to help better manage our expectations:

- Understand that this is Plan A
- Expect thorns and thistles
- Expect to be pruned

Which of these ideas, if any, are new thoughts for you? How will you think differently in the second half as a result?

ELEVEN

A Brush with Tragedy—When the Nature of Life Is Tragic

My God, my God, why have you forsaken me?
PSALM 22:1, QUOTED BY JESUS

IN THE BASEBALL MOVIE *FIELD OF Dreams* Ray Kinsella and Terrance Mann drive a Volkswagen minibus to a small Midwestern town to find Archie "Moonlight" Graham.

Decades earlier, for a brief flash of glory, "Moonlight" Graham was brought up to the majors, but played just one inning—and never got to bat. When they found him, Ray, played by Kevin Costner, asked him, "What was it like?"

"Moonlight," now a doctor portrayed by Burt Lancaster, held his thumb and index finger close together, squinted, and said, "It was like having it this close to your dreams, and then you watch them brush past you like a stranger in a crowd.

"At the time you don't think that much of it. You know, we just don't recognize the most significant moments of our lives when they're happening. Back then I thought there would be other days. I didn't realize then that that was the only day."

After a long, suspended moment to absorb the full meaning of what had been said, Ray asked, "What's your wish?"

"It will have to stay a wish. I was born here. I lived here. I'll die here. No regrets," said Archie, smiling broadly.

Incredulous, Ray said, "Fifty years ago you came so close. I mean, it would kill some men to get that close to their dream and not touch it. They would consider it a tragedy."

"If I only would have gotten to be a doctor for five minutes, now that would have been a tragedy," Archie replied, eyes twinkling.

Later, back at his motel, Ray discussed the extraordinary exchange with Terrance Mann, played by James Earl Jones. "So maybe we're not supposed to take him with us. Now I don't know why we are here," he mused.

Terrance said ponderously, "Maybe it was to find out if one inning can change the world."

"Do you think it did?" asked Ray.

"Well," said Terrance, "it did for these people. If he had gotten a hit he would have stayed in baseball."[1]

Archie "Moonlight" Graham lived a life that mattered. It was exactly the life he was supposed to live. True, his first dream died. But his second dream turned out even better. He did change the world, and so have you.

By midlife we each have endured half a dozen or more major tests. Some of these tests turned tragic.

Have you thought of what's happened in your life as a tragedy? In reality, a loving, gracious and sovereign God is working all things together for the good of those who love him.[2] Who's to say what is tragedy and what is not? Wherever you have landed in life, you have landed for a reason. What we often take for tragedy is only disappointment. How can we tell the difference?

WHAT QUALIFIES AS TRAGEDY?

What is the difference between a disappointment and a tragedy?

While I doubt we can find a single line to separate them, the main difference between disappointment and tragedy would be a matter of scale. Disappointments are frustrations—your picnic gets rained on. Tragedies are disasters—someone is struck by lightning. One is minor; the other major.

Often we mistake our disappointments for tragedies. Even when something does qualify as tragedy, it often turns to blessing later. And many times, tragedy strengthens rather than weakens.

When our daughter was in middle school she suffered a disappointment that at the time she took as tragedy. She had attended cheerleading tryouts for the junior varsity squad with her classmates.

When the phone call came, she was devastated to hear, "I'm sorry, Jen. You didn't make it." She then learned that all of her best friends did make it.

She sobbed and sobbed. Her friend (and later college roommate), Melanie, happened to be at our home when the call came. We all tried to comfort her. We even took her out for pizza.

"I don't understand why. I really did my best," she said. "I'm the only one of my friends who didn't make it. Do you know what this means? I can't go to cheerleading camp. I can't go on the road trips. I practiced for three months. How can I try so hard and just not make it? The whole next year—it's going to be so different now!"

Jen was offered, however, a position on the middle school squad. We were quite proud of her when she decided to cheer, even though her best friends and classmates were on the junior varsity squad.

The following year she and her friends all tried out for the varsity cheerleading squad. This time, all her friends made varsity except her. To her credit, when offered a slot on the junior varsity squad she took it. Again, for the entire year she cheered for the junior varsity squad while all of her best buddies cheered for the varsity.

The following year she again tried out for varsity and finally made it. No one who ever cheered for her school has appreciated the privilege more than our beloved daughter. Her character deepened so much through this adversity. Her confidence bloomed because she didn't give up and quit. What looked like a tragedy was really only a disappointment and, in the end, turned out to be a blessing.

Who's to say if a thing is a tragedy or not? Give it time. No tragedy is beyond the grace of God. Even when true tragedy devastates us, God will bring good out of it. "I will repay you for the years the locusts have eaten," says the Lord (Joel 2:25).

A PERSPECTIVE ON TRAGEDY

One day I went inside a gas station to pay. A particularly attractive young girl was working the counter. Her entire jaw, however, was a mass of brutally scarred tissue. I asked her how it happened. She said, "When I was two a neighbor's German shepherd attacked me."

Walking back to my car I was overcome with emotion, pondering how those few tragic seconds disfigured not only this woman's face, but all her hopes and dreams. I wept as I pulled out of the station.

The nature of life is tragic. Each day our ministries will take us to places of loneliness, despair, death, fear, brokenness, exhaustion, emptiness, evil, pain, and persecutions. The world is full of death and decay.

However, the nature of the kingdom is "righteousness, peace and joy in the Holy Spirit" (Romans 14:17). Though we are associated with tragedy much of the time, our lives are not tragic.

Rather, we are agents of the kingdom—Christ's ambassadors. We bring life where there is death; light where there is darkness; hope where there is despair.

A physician's office is a gathering place for the sick. How would you feel, though, if you went to your doctor and were greeted by a depressed and mopey receptionist, taken to an examining room by an assistant with a deep hacking cough, and had your vital signs taken by a nurse who was pale and emaciated? You would run!

The problem, of course, is that we are all subject to the daily aches and pains of living in a world held hostage by sin. Yet, if we, his ambassadors, appear without hope there can be no hope. Because we have the kingdom we must be cheerful receptionists, sympathetic assistants, and joyful, competent nurses to people touched by tragedy.

What message do you send? Is it the message of reconciliation? Above all else, our lives should pulsate with the love of Christ—the Great Physician—"as though God were making his appeal through us." He has a purpose for our lives. We are ambassadors of the kingdom, not pallbearers of the kingdom.

As Tom Skinner said, God calls us to become the live demonstration of what's happening in heaven. That way, anytime someone wants to know what's happening there, all they have to do is check with us. We are to become to each other what we want our communities to become. That will create a model so attractive that people will want to be part of it.

God is building a family, a community of people who love God with all their hearts and love one another as themselves. This family is called the church. Then, when someone needs to see the doctor, we can help minister to their need with joyful encouragement.

THE DIFFICULT DECADES

For over twenty-two years I have met weekly with a man for accountability and fellowship. We began meeting when he was fifty-eight and I was twenty-eight. When I turned thirty he said, "The twenties were the toughest years. Now that you've gotten past them everything should be just fine." That really ministered to me, because the twenties had been hard.

One day not long after I turned forty he said, "The thirties—now those are the really tough years. Once you get past them everything is smooth sailing."

I said, "Hold the phone, here! That's what you told me ten years ago when I turned thirty. I suppose when I turn fifty you're going to tell me the forties were the toughest years."

Having obviously forgotten his comment from ten years earlier, he laughed and said, "Well, you're probably right. Actually, every decade is difficult in its own way."

JOSEPH'S DIFFICULT DECADES

If you never heard the end of Joseph's life, you would go away thinking his life had been tragic. Joseph was a dreamer with a dream. You know the story. A daring dream, a terrible tragedy, a tremendous triumph.

Hated by his brothers enough that they wanted to kill him, Joseph was sold as a slave. He rose in the ranks to handle the business affairs of his master. His master's wife seduced him and then falsely accused him of rape. He was thrown into prison and forgotten. Some years later Joseph miraculously interpreted Pharaoh's dream. He became the number-two man in Egypt.

The Bible makes no mention of Joseph ever complaining. The only early clues we find about how he feels are the names of his two sons:

> Joseph named his firstborn Manasseh and said, "It is because
> God has made me forget all my trouble and all my father's

household." The second son he named Ephraim and said, "It is because God has made me fruitful in the land of my suffering" (Genesis 41:51–52).

Just about the time Joseph was able to put all of the tragic things that had happened behind him, his brothers showed up. They had come to buy grain during a famine.

The pain of his tragedy began to boil. By the time the brothers came back again with his blood brother, Benjamin, Joseph couldn't control himself any longer. He had everyone leave his presence but them, then made himself known to his incredulous brothers. He wept so loudly that everyone knew about it. Joseph had an emotion explosion!

What was it that Joseph understood at thirty-nine years of age? At the midpoint of his life, in an instant of divine clarity, he understood the God-purpose behind his tragic circumstances. Everything fell into place. God had been sovereignly orchestrating the seemingly random circumstances of his life.

The same is true for you. God is sovereignly orchestrating the seemingly random circumstances of your life. What does this mean if it is true? It means you can trust him.

Over a few brief days, the last three pieces of the puzzle that explained Joseph's pain fell into place. The first puzzle piece was that pain became explainable. Joseph was a man in deep emotional pain. Here was a man highly successful in the world, yet from a dysfunctional family. He had suffered deeply because of his family; he had been torn from his family; he had buried the painful thought of his family. And now that wound was ripped open, and the festering poison oozed out in a healing way.

What Joseph finally saw was that nothing that happened to him by human will happened apart from God's will. And that's the lesson for us. Our pain is explainable. Nothing that has happened to you by human will has happened to you apart from God's will. That's because God is sovereignly orchestrating the seemingly random circumstances of your life.

The second piece of the puzzle was that purpose became visible. Joseph had an "aha!" To his brothers he said, "Now I see what God was doing! God sent me here ahead of you. I was sent here to save your lives. So then, it was not you who did this, but God. You sold me in hatred;

God sent me to Egypt to save you. You meant it for harm, God meant it for good."

Joseph realized what God's purpose was behind all the suffering. God had raised Joseph to such a great height in Egypt "for such a time as this." God had blessed him for his faithfulness, to be sure, but also for a purpose larger than his own well-being. He is the sovereign God who orchestrates evil for good. It is God's will and not human will that is the controlling reality of our lives.

What Joseph saw was that his life was not his own. He understood that the interests of a single life must fit into the larger context of redemptive history. We have all experienced the frustration on not knowing why. This is why: God is working all things out in accordance with the purpose of his will.

The third puzzle piece that fell into place for Joseph was that peace became possible. When Joseph finally understood that what happened to him was a "God thing" more than a "man thing" he was able to forgive. A reconciliation took place. When Joseph saw that God was in charge he could forgive. When we, too, perceive the sovereign hand of God working in our circumstances we are able to forgive others.

God is sovereignly orchestrating the seemingly random circumstances of our lives. When we understand this, pain becomes explainable, purpose becomes visible, and peace becomes possible.

FAITH BUILDERS

I know from my own tragedies how difficult it is to trust in God when it seems he is the one crushing you. Our consolation in our tragedies is to know that God is good, and you can trust him. What will give us second wind for the second half is to have faith that the God who sovereignly orchestrates the seemingly random circumstances of our lives actually loves us. So I would like to close this chapter by offering you a number of ways to understand faith. I hope you enjoy them.

- Faith is believing God in the face of unbelievable circumstances.
- Faith is believing my Bible when it makes no sense, humanly speaking.

- Faith is relying on the authority of Scripture over my own best thinking.
- Faith is letting the reality of the unseen rule over the unreality of the seen.
- Faith is subordinating the tumult I feel in my emotions to that previous decision I made in my will to trust Jesus.
- Faith is believing God will do every single thing he has promised in his perfect time.
- Faith is not trusting God where he has not promised, but where he has.
- Faith is believing God will supply all my needs and that in the chambers of his private counsel he has measured my need on the scales of mercy.
- Faith is continuing to believe, trust, and wait when the hot, scorching breath of adversity blows unrelentingly across the landscape of my circumstances.
- Faith is not, not, not a leap into the dark; but a careful, reasoned step into the glorious Light that sets us free from bondage to sin, decay, and death.

Be encouraged. Though we brush against tragedy, our lives are not tragic. We can have faith because of his inseparable love for us.

The Bible puts it this way: "Who shall separate us from the love of Christ? ... For I am convinced that neither death nor life, neither angels nor demons, neither the present nor the future, nor any powers, neither height nor depth, nor anything else in all creation, will be able to separate us from the love of God that is in Christ Jesus our Lord" (Romans 8:35, 38–39).

FOCUS QUESTIONS

1. What was your dream that didn't come true? Do you have regrets about it? Explain your answer.
2. What have been your major tests in life? Which of them turned out tragic? Which of them, while disappointing, turned out for a greater good?

3. The Bible states a principle of God addressed to those who love him: "I will repay you for the years the locusts have eaten" (Joel 2:25). In what ways have you seen this true in your own life?

4. While we are all subject to the aches and pains of life, we are also called to be Christ's ambassadors. Because we have the kingdom we must be cheerful receptionists, sympathetic assistants, and joyful, competent nurses to people touched by tragedy. What message do you send? Is it the message of reconciliation to God?

5. Joseph was middle-aged. He suffered tragedy. His life was restored. God "restored the years the locusts have eaten." He told his brothers, "You meant it for evil but God meant it for good." Two questions:

   • Have you been able to see your tragedies the way Joseph saw his, and why or why not?

   • Have you been able to forgive those who have caused your pain like Joseph did, and why or why not? What is a practical step you can take?

6. Look again at the list of faith definitions under the subheading "Faith Builders." Which of these do you find interesting? Difficult? Do you have faith to believe that God is sovereignly orchestrating the seemingly random circumstances of your life for good? Explain your answer.

TWELVE

Leftover Pain—How God Uses Sorrows That Won't Go Away

At the same time, you need to know I carry with me at all times a huge sorrow. It's an enormous pain deep within me, and I'm never free of it.

PAUL, ROMANS 9:1–2, *THE MESSAGE*

JACK AND EDIE HAVE A DAUGHTER boys don't find attractive, so she doesn't get asked on dates. When it came time for her college's Sadie Hawkins dance she screwed up her courage to ask a boy she liked. Her dorm hall friends gathered around as she placed the call. When she asked he apparently said yes, because she squealed, "You will?" The girls laughed. Later, he canceled.

A woman with beautiful long blonde hair recalled an occasion in high school when she was walking down a sidewalk. Several boys in a car pulled up from behind, but when they saw her face they laughed and roared off.

Some pains are considerably more tragic than others.

From our earliest memories to this very day we each must live with pain that won't go away. But how do we cope with this residue of leftover pain? Whether it's a permanent problem or the residual of past hurts, God has a purpose for your pain.

Our sufferings go through stages: First, we absorb the blow of disappointment. Next, we deny that we are really hurting. Then, we cry out in anguish, pound the table with our fists, and rage against the injustice. Finally, we quiet ourselves before a holy God and make peace with our pain. Only then, can we move on.

In this chapter we will see how God gives us second wind to serve him out of our defeats. We will see how God uses leftover pain to reach more and more people.

THE PROBLEM THAT WON'T GO AWAY

Do you have a problem that won't go away? Perhaps it is a child who will never be that bright. Maybe you or your spouse face a lifelong health challenge. Perhaps you have been chronically underemployed. Possibly family members think your faith is a joke.

Why would a gracious and loving God allow us to have problems that won't go away?

The apostle Paul had a problem that wouldn't go away:

"To keep me from becoming conceited because of these surpassingly great revelations, there was given me a thorn in my flesh, a messenger of Satan, to torment me. Three times I pleaded with the Lord to take it away from me. But he said to me, 'My grace is sufficient for you, for my power is made perfect in weakness'" (2 Corinthians 12:7–9).

Paul had a problem and God wanted to help. Paul's problem was a temptation to conceit. Conceit, or pride, in this context means "to raise oneself over, to become haughty." In order to keep Paul from a problem he struggled to resist—becoming conceited—God gave him another problem he couldn't solve—a thorn in his flesh.

What was the problem Paul couldn't solve? We don't know. Suggestions have ranged from earache to headache (Tertullian), a specific enemy (Chrysostom), some bodily pain (Augustine), impure temptations of the flesh (Luther), some affliction of the eyes, a recurring fever, a speech impediment, and even epilepsy, to name a few.[1]

It doesn't matter. That's not the point the Scriptures want to make. Kindly, God has left this "thorn" unnamed so we may each project our own "thorn"—that problem that won't go away—into the text and find comfort.

While we don't know what Paul's thorn was, we do know that it "tormented" him. To torment used this way literally means, "to rap with the fist." Paul is being humbled by severe means. Why? Again, to keep him from becoming conceited.

As we all do when plagued by a problem, Paul asked God to take away his thorn in the flesh. If you have a problem, by all means ask God to remove it. He may kindly answer your prayer. But in this case, God chose to leave Paul's problem rather than remove it:

"Three times I pleaded with the Lord to take it away from me. But he said to me, 'My grace is sufficient for you, for my power is made perfect in weakness'" (2 Corinthians 12:8–9).

Is this an act of cruelty by God? No. Instead, God delivered Paul from a strength he could not handle by giving him a weakness that wouldn't go away.

Why would God leave you with a "thorn in the flesh"—a problem that won't go away? Does he do it to be cruel? No. Rather, God in his grace and kindness is working out everything for your good (and his) in ways known only to the secret counsel of his holy, infinite, divine mind.

The message for us is simple: To protect you from a strength you can't handle, God may bless you with a weakness that won't go away.

If you are a capable person, have money, and are good at your work, will this lead to humility? If you are a strong Christian, rich in good deeds, and morally pure, will this lead to humility?

Every strength is a temptation to pride and self-sufficiency. For Paul the strength that tempted him was spiritual knowledge. For me it is my organization and self-discipline. What is it for you? This is a good thing to know. For most of us, the sins of our piety far exceed the sins of our immorality.

Teacher Paul Miller suggested that the more we grow in Christ the bigger the cross needs to become, not smaller. The longer you are a Christian the greater your capacity for self-righteousness (pride) grows. The sequence is, "I've learned more, therefore I know more, therefore I make fewer mistakes, therefore I have less to learn from other Christians."

The formula could be presented this way: Biblical Truth + My Experience = A Complete Inability to Listen and a Complete Ignorance of that Inability. Miller calls the result "unteachability." A problem that won't go away will keep you teachable.

Miller goes on to correctly say that more love and knowledge of Jesus will result in more success. But the more success you have the more you begin to believe deep down that there is something intrinsically in you that produced it. A problem that won't go away keeps us focused on the Lord and not ourselves.

Paul didn't like his thorn—he asked three times for its removal. But he could accept it when God told him, "My grace is sufficient for you, for my power is made perfect in weakness." This is a message for us too. Whatever your thorn, his grace is sufficient for your comfort.

Eventually, Paul came to realize that what at first appeared to be a curse was actually a blessing. That's because God told him, "My power (or strength) is made perfect in weakness." In other words, God's strength displays itself best when it doesn't have to share credit with human strength. When this light finally broke on Paul he exclaimed, "Therefore I will boast all the more gladly about my weaknesses, so that Christ's power may rest on me. That is why, for Christ's sake, I delight in weaknesses, in insults, in hardships, in persecutions, in difficulties. For when I am weak, then I am strong" (2 Corinthians 12:9–10).

Failing deliverance, Paul "boasted" (or gloried) in his infirmities. Why? "So that Christ's power may rest on me." It's ironic: The source of Paul's power was Christ, but the method by which it came was through "weakness" not strength. Isn't it amazing how often God's way is exactly the opposite of what we would think up on our own?

Once Paul grasped the truth that his "thorn" would be made bearable by the sufficiency of God's grace, he took delight in every difficult thing that happened to him. But notice that he said, "For Christ's sake, I delight." Even here we have a temptation for self-righteousness and pious pride. But Paul gives the glory for handling all his problems to Christ. So should we.

For Paul, weakness became the source of his strength: "For when I am weak, then I am strong." He saw how God displays his power better through a weak dependent vessel than a strong independent vessel.

These were Paul's responses. These should be our responses, too, once we accept that God has given us a problem that won't go away. Remember, to protect you from a strength you can't handle, God may bless you with a weakness that won't go away. This is grace. Let us fix our eyes not on our thorn, but on the sufficiency of God's grace.

PAIN IS OUR TEACHER

In a previous chapter I mentioned the pain of being passed over as a Promise Keepers speaker. At the midpoint of my adult life I have a dozen other equal or greater major disappointments. You have yours.

A friend owns a heavy construction company with a large international emphasis. He called one day about a joint venture he had undertaken a year earlier to pursue construction projects in an Asian country with what he described as several "high pedigree" companies. His only stipulation in joining the venture had been that there be no bribes.

After a year of work on this project he got wind that their agent was paying bribes to government officials. He was distraught. He had tied up a huge amount of time and money to get this far.

He said, "I've called all my partners, and I'm the only one in the joint venture who has a problem with this. In fact, one of my own people said to me, 'I don't see the principle this violates.' It's not the money that makes this so complicated—it's the relationships." Knowing his character, I believed him.

He asked for my opinion. From experience I know that a made-up mind is almost impossible to change. So I first wanted to learn whether he truly wanted counsel or merely support for a decision he had already made. I asked, "What do you think God is saying to you?"

"I don't want to be Western," he began. "I want to be Christian. My heart and my mind say it's wrong. I've read the Scriptures. I feel like I know God's will, but I've got so much at stake here. Don't I have a bigger responsibility to my partners? How do I testify to God now?"

This was an excruciating, very real problem. He felt the weight of his relationships deeply. He felt the gravity of his integrity even heavier.

We all must make painful decisions. Sometimes to do the right thing seemingly hurts more than doing the wrong thing. God wants to use this pain to teach us.

In the end my friend withdrew from the joint venture. To make matters worse, a week later another agent representing another Asian joint venture called to say they had been awarded a magnificent contract, but it would require some bribes to government officials. In this first instance they were still seeking business. Now, the deal was in hand.

My friend said, "I'm sorry, but I'm not going to pay any bribes." The agent immediately hopped a plane from Asia to my friend's office in the southeastern United States. For the better part of a day the agent tried to persuade my friend to change his mind. At one point the agent had to fight back tears. My friend stuck to his position.

These two experiences unraveled his company's Asian strategy. They lost significant money and wasted a lot of time. He kept his integrity but at a huge economic sacrifice. The accusations have stopped. The chaos of unwinding the joint ventures has settled down. Things have returned to normal. They are now considering several promising South American projects.

Here's the issue: What does he do with the leftover pain? And more to the point, after you have worked through your major letdowns what do *you* do with the leftover pain? It may be an empty nest, a divorce, a bitter career setback, a financial calamity, or a death in the family. Sometimes the simple memory of the past pulsates with pain. What is its purpose? How can we use it constructively? Can it give us a second wind?

Pain is for growth. Pain drives us forward or backward. Pain refocuses us. God sovereignly uses pain to redirect our steps. And as we will see, pain is the grace of God that is reaching more and more people.

Here's a postscript to the story. Not much later the Asian economy suffered a meltdown, and those who had invested in construction projects took huge losses. This helped my friend to see how gracious God can be—how God honors those who honor him. Because he chose the high-but-painful road, he was later spared an even greater pain. Isn't God good, after all? Who really knows if a thing is bad or not? Given time we tend to see God's grace.

Leftover pain is the grace of God that teaches us

- who we are
- whose we are
- who the purpose of our life is
- what the purpose of our life is

PAIN TEACHES US OUR IDENTITY

From the age of twenty-six to forty severe allergies to both inhalants and foods debilitated me. I've never been tested for anything to which I'm not allergic, except the glycerin fluid in which the allergens were mixed for testing. My chief symptom was migraines, which occurred almost daily. My head would pound, my insides would churn, and all my muscles would ache.

One day Patsy gave me an article on migraines she had run across. As I sat in our family room reading the article, I began to sob as every sentence I read described me.

Over the years I pled with God to spare me. I would review my behavior and attitudes to see what I may have done wrong. Over and over and over again, I looked for a spiritual reason behind the daily attacks. At first I was introspective. *Am I doing something wrong? Am I being punished for past sins? Am I missing some spiritual secret?*

After my patience ran out I became strident with God. *Where are You, God, when it hurts? If You love me, why won't You deliver me from these crippling attacks? Is God really God? Are You really there? If You are there, do You care? Do You even know? If You know, then You must not care. If You care, then You must not be able to do anything about it.*

Years later God had never answered one on my interrogatives, not one of my complaints. But I had changed. I moved from needing an answer to simply needing God. I moved from insisting on a healing to submission to his will. I learned to submit myself and trust that he is good. I stopped accusing God and fell at his feet in praise and adoration.

My pain taught me to find my identity in God and God alone. Before, my identity was tied to how I was doing in business, what my peers thought of me, and making progress toward my goals.

But pain taught me something about identity. My pain showed me that "who I am" does not depend on any outward circumstance, but only on my relationship with the sovereign Creator God. We belong to God. We have been bought with a price. Our lives are not our own.

As I have written before, we cannot fully know *who* we are until we know *Whose* we are. Once we know to Whom we belong, we are set free to establish our true identity. Pain focuses our thoughts to that end.

PAIN TEACHES US OUR PURPOSE

My pain also taught me to find my purpose in God and God alone. Before, my purpose was tied to an image I pictured of myself as a successful businessman at a certain level of achievement. We each have some "vision" or "image" of ourselves that controls, or directs, our behavior. For me, every gesture, word, action, decision, and minute was moderated by my purpose.

But pain taught me something about purpose. My pain showed me that "why I exist" does not relate to my own ambitions, but rather to the will of Almighty God. He has a plan for our lives—a purpose. He is a God of purpose, and he wants to use us in a perfect way as his servants.

We cannot fully know *what* our purpose is until we know *Who* our purpose is. The more we know him, the more we will know what to do. Leftover pain leads us to more deeply consider and yield to God's will and purpose for us. Notice how it is put in the Scriptures: "Therefore, since Christ suffered in his body, arm yourselves also with the same attitude, because he who has suffered in his body is done with sin. As a result, he does not live the rest of his earthly life for evil human desires, but rather for the will of God" (1 Peter 4:1–2).

Actually, this passage was a salve to my migraine torments. Yes, Christ did suffer in his body. Yet he willingly suffered, "Not my will but your will be done." The Bible encourages us to take the same approach.

Experientially, you and I both know that when we are sick or suffering in some way in our bodies, the last thing that looks appealing to us is sin. Through repeated sufferings our spirits become deadened toward sin. Sin is always crouching at our door, but we find we make progress through suffering.

The one who suffers in his body "does not live the rest of his earthly life for evil human desires, but rather for the will of God." Isn't this, at the end of the day, what we each desperately long to achieve—the will of God? So then, pain is not a curse, but a blessing. It shows us *Whose* we are and *Who* is the purpose of our lives. Knowing this liberates us to also know *who* we are and *what* is the purpose of our lives.

PAIN REACHES PEOPLE

Paul had many pains beside his thorn in the flesh.

"But we have this treasure in jars of clay to show that this all-surpassing power is from God and not from us. We are hard pressed on every side, but not crushed; perplexed, but not in despair; persecuted, but not abandoned; struck down, but not destroyed" (2 Corinthians 4:7–9).

Paul understood that the ultimate reason for his leftover pain in the "jar of clay" (his body) was to show God's power to a watching world. Here is a modern-day example.

A seventy-eight-year-old man underwent extensive hand surgery. The recuperation period was lengthy and painful. The young physical therapist working with him afterward said, "Where do you get your happiness from?"

"Why do you ask?" he responded.

"Well, all my other clients seem so beat down by their problems. But you're different. It occurred to me that I would be wise to learn your secret now while I'm still in my twenties."

In the moments that followed he was able to share how God has changed his life through Christ.

We should never go looking for pain and troubles. And we should never keep pain and troubles at our side when we can peaceably put them away. Nevertheless, when we do have pain, God will use it to reach people. Of the many troubles Paul mentioned in the verse above, he said, "All this is for your benefit, so that *the grace that is reaching more and more people* may cause thanksgiving to overflow to the glory of God" (2 Corinthians 4:15, italics added).

There is purpose for our leftover pain. It teaches us our identity and purpose. God uses it to bring glory to himself. He uses it to bring a living message to a dying world. The problem that won't go away is a blessing, not a curse. Let us, therefore, fix our eyes toward our real home.

"Therefore we do not lose heart. Though outwardly we are wasting away, yet inwardly we are being renewed day by day. For our light and momentary troubles are achieving for us an eternal glory that far outweighs them all. So we fix our eyes not on what is seen, but on what is

unseen. For what is seen is temporary, but what is unseen is eternal"
(2 Corinthians 4:16–18).

FOCUS QUESTIONS

1. The apostle Paul said, "I carry with me at all times a huge sorrow. It's an enormous pain deep within me, and I'm never free of it" (Romans 9:1–2 THE MESSAGE). Do you relate to Paul and, if so, how?
2. Where do you still feel leftover pain from your past? Why do you think you still feel pain? Is your pain of a nature that it would be best to put it behind you, and why or why not?
3. "To protect you from a strength you can't handle, God may bless you with a weakness that won't go away." Do you agree or not, and why?
4. "God in his grace and kindness is working out everything for your good (and his) in ways known only to the secret counsel of his holy, infinite, divine mind." Do you agree or not? Should this be a sufficient answer for us, and why or why not?
5. How has pain helped you discover your identity? How has pain helped you discover your purpose? How has pain helped you to reach out to others?

PART 3

Reinventing Yourself for the Second Half

THIRTEEN

Second-Half Success—Recalibrating How You Measure Accomplishment

Make no little plans. They have no magic to stir men's blood.

DANIEL H. BURNHAM, ON DEVISING
CHICAGO'S PLAN OF 1909

A MIDDLE-AGED LEE SAID, "I SEE what's happened to my parents in their later years. They have not finished well. I really want to rethink my life. I want to make sure I spend the rest of my life in a way that counts."

Unmistakably, the biggest desire of midlife is, "I want the rest of my life to count." I would like us to consider for a moment the questions "How do you measure success?" and "What determines success for you?" The answers we give determine whether our lives will count in a way that really matters.

THE PROBLEM

Imagine three different high school basketball coaches. They each have similar personalities, temperaments, and coaching styles. Yet even similar people doing the same work will have widely different results. The question is, what makes one person different from another? The answer lies in differing motives. In other words, how do we measure success? Our motives determine to what we give priority.

Take our three coaches. A consuming desire to build character motivates the first coach. For him, that's what determines success or failure. So he prioritizes everything he does to build integrity, discipline, teamwork, and leadership qualities into his players.

Winning the state championship animates the second coach. This affects who he recruits to the team and how. It determines playing time and how he treats players in the locker room. It also creates a high-performance atmosphere. For this coach winning defines whether or not he is successful.

A passion to find a full or partial scholarship to play ball in college for as many of his players as possible drives the third coach. That's success for him. It pushes him to maintain a huge network of scouts. He constantly phones coaches to send someone to see his players. He sets priorities based on what will bring him this success.

These are three outwardly similar coaches with completely different inward motivations. These coaches will each obtain a different result with their lives. Ironically, it's possible to live your entire life based upon a motivation of which you are only scarcely aware.

THE NEXT TEN YEARS

Are you in touch with how you measure success? Can you give a precise statement of what determines success for you? If so, take the time to write it down now.

What does your statement say about your underlying motivations? Let me encourage you to pause and contemplate two questions:

- If over the next ten years you get exactly what you want, will it make you happy?
- If you keep doing what you're doing and things work out over the next ten years, will you be able to look back and say, "I've led a significant life?"

If yes, terrific. If you can't unreservedly answer yes, what specifically is missing?

For the rest of this chapter I would like to focus on five shifts in attitude that can create a warmer, more hospitable second half. These five dispositions are the "software" of success in the second half.

FROM WINNING TO FINISHING

Success in the first half is winning; success in the second half is finishing and helping someone else finish too.

Joni Eareckson Tada attended the Los Angeles Special Olympics one day with her husband, Ken, who volunteers for the games.

Six mentally handicapped contestants lined up by the starting blocks for a fifty-yard race. A sunny Down's syndrome girl with thick glasses jumped up and down. One little boy kicked the dirt. Another waved to his family in the stands.

The starter gun went "bang," and the six contestants bobbed and wove down the track. Suddenly, one of the Down's syndrome boys hopped the curb and started to run toward his friends in the infield. Joni's husband, Ken, tried in vain to "reroute" the boy.

Just then the Down's syndrome girl with thick glasses spotted him. She stopped a few yards short of the finish line and called to him as the other contestants passed her by. "Hey, over here! This way!" When he didn't come, she ran over to where he stood, linked arms with him, and led him back onto the track. Then they finished the race together arm in arm. The other runners, who had long ago finished, greeted them with hugs. The crowd, now standing, alternately fought back tears or cheered.[1]

By midlife we see that the goal of life is not merely winning. We see the beauty of finishing well and helping others to do the same. Success in the second half helps others.

In *Habits of the Heart*, Robert Bellah notes that very few people have found a life devoted to "personal ambition and consumerism" rewarding. Instead, most people seek in one way or another to transcend the limitations of a self-centered life. We often hear of the selfish, narcissistic "me generation" in America. Bellah has heard it too, but according to his research, if those people are out there in large numbers he could not find them.[2]

FROM PRESSURE ZONE TO COMFORT ZONE

Success in the first half creates a pressure zone; success in the second half finds a comfort zone.

A forty-nine-year-old man asked me to have lunch. He explained that over twenty-five years he had built a highly successful, debt-free specialty magazine publishing company. He had an unusual opportunity to acquire a much larger, complementary publishing company. To make the purchase, however, would require financing. To secure the loan he would have to pledge his existing free-and-clear company and all of his personal assets, including his home, as collateral.

He was looking for advice. I asked him two questions. First, "David, if you had no obligations, unlimited resources, and could do anything you wanted with your life—what would you do?"

He said, "Pat, I'm living my dream. Every morning when I wake up I can't wait to see what the day may bring. Actually, I have a management team that pretty much runs the company, so I can spend more than half my time in ministry and community service."

Second question: "David, why would you want to make this change?"

He said, "Pat, there is one and only one reason I'm considering this deal. I have eight ambitious young managers I've brought into the business and trained. I'm afraid that if I don't provide them growth opportunities they may leave."

"So, let me get this straight," I said. "You are living your dream, and the only reason you are considering this acquisition is for the benefit of your managers?"

"Yes," he said. "That's right."

I was dumbfounded but managed to continue. "So, if I understand this correctly, you have spent twenty-five years to build a well-oiled, highly profitable business that you own debt-free. You are considering whether or not to risk a lifetime of toil on a single transaction that bets not only your company but all of the personal wealth you have accumulated in your forty-nine years of life.

"Meanwhile, you are doing this at the very moment you are living your dream and have plenty of free time to devote to other causes. And if I understand you correctly, the sole reason you are doing this is to please your key employees. Do I understand this correctly?"

In David's defense, he knew he was too close to the trees to see the forest. The entire reason he asked me to lunch was that he was suspicious about forging ahead. He was already leaning toward not going ahead with it. As you may suspect, David ended up passing on this opportunity. Yet how many of us would have forged ahead anyway?

I wonder how different our lives would be if we would visualize the action we propose as a newspaper article before we actually did it. If only we would take time to write out the script of the decision we're considering, we would often see how ludicrous our thinking is.

Midlife should certainly be a time of spreading our wings and trying new things. Yet, these adventures should not jeopardize the foundations we spent twenty or more years to lay. A famous singer was once asked the secret of how she had maintained her voice so many years. She replied, "You must learn to sing off the interest and not the principal." We should give careful thought before spending "the principal" of the first half on second-half dreams. They could turn into nightmares.

God has made us for a comfort zone—a place not found by flailing ambitions and ever-increasing pressures. Instead, the Bible exhorts, "Make it your ambition to lead a quiet life, to mind your own business and to work with your hands, just as we told you, so that your daily life may win the respect of outsiders and so that you will not be dependent on anybody" (1 Thessalonians 4:11–12).

FROM IN A HURRY TO TAKING YOUR TIME

Success in the first half is in a hurry; success in the second half takes its time.

We recently had an electrical problem that several service calls could not correct. Finally, the rather large company said, "We're going to send you our best man." At first I thought, *Now you're talking!* Then it occurred to me: *Why didn't you do that in the first place!*

When the electrician came out I followed him around like a lost puppy. I really wanted to know what made him their best man. He didn't seem particularly special or unique. Finally, curiosity got the best of me and I said, "They tell me you're the best man the company's got. What makes you so good?"

He chuckled and said, "Well, I don't know about all that, but when I do my work I take my time."

"I take my time." When we lose the physical vigor to repeat our work two or three times, we can substitute the wisdom of taking enough time to do it right once.

FROM THE MASTER PLAN TO THE MASTER'S PLAN

Success in the first half is to pursue a master plan; success in the second half is to work on The Master's Plan.

A key halftime issue is whether or not we will fully surrender our lives to the plan for which the Master designed us. Many pursue a master plan, but not The Master's Plan. Here's the difference:

the master plan brings:	The Master's Plan offers:
accomplishment	Accomplishment
comfort	Comfort
contentment	Contentment

Why settle for "lowercase" living? Learn—and accept—God's design for your life. Too often we're interested in the success of our goal. God's interested in the success of our soul. How good it is to be able to accept our lot in life: "So I saw that there is nothing better for a man than to enjoy his work, because that is his lot. For who can bring him to see what will happen after him?" (Ecclesiastes 3:22).

"Then I realized that it is good and proper for a man to eat and drink, and to find satisfaction in his toilsome labor under the sun during the few days of life God has given him—for this is his lot. Moreover, when God gives any man wealth and possessions, and enables him to enjoy them, to accept his lot and be happy in his work—this is a gift of God" (Ecclesiastes 5:18–19).

FROM MAXIMIZING TO OPTIMIZING

Success in the first half is maximizing; success in the second half is optimizing.

Over several years a man's boss kept asking him to stay later and later, then for several more years to come in earlier and earlier. When the man finally stepped back to evaluate, he realized he was working seventy hours a week. He wondered, "Is the price I'm paying for success worth it?"

In the first half virtually everyone in our generation starved for the American Dream. We hungered to "maximize" our success. As one man put it, "My problem is that I want it all." To maximize means "to pursue the greatest possible quantity." It seemed natural to every young person in our generation to see how far and high they might achieve. For most of us it was "experimental." We found "our" right level and settled down. To some, however, maximizing becomes obsession.

At the midpoint the question to ask becomes, "How can I *optimize* my success?" To optimize means "to make the most effective use of something." Optimizing implies restraint and balance, best achieved through living by priorities.

CONCLUSION

In the first half we were driven by motivations that may or may not have made us happy. We often live in a pressure zone, work on our own agendas, find ourselves in too much of a hurry, and try to extract the maximum out of everything.

We need a second wind. Second wind for the second half will come when we transition into a comfort zone that suits our temperament, slow down and take our time, seek The Master's Plan, and learn how to optimize.

FOCUS QUESTIONS

1. What has been the basic motivation of your life? How satisfied are you with your answer?
2. How did you define success in the first half? Be specific. If you did not already do so earlier in the chapter, write down a precise statement of what determines success for you.
3. If you did not already do so earlier in the chapter, let me encourage you to pause and contemplate two questions:

   • If over the next ten years you get exactly what you want, will it make you happy?
   • If you keep doing what you're doing and things work out over the next ten years, will you be able to look back and say, "I've led a significant life?"

If yes, terrific. If you can't unreservedly answer yes, what specifically is missing?

4. Which of the ideas presented in this chapter triggered new thoughts?

- From winning to finishing
- From pressure zone to comfort zone
- From in a hurry to taking your time
- From a master plan to The Master's Plan
- From maximizing to optimizing

5. What are one or two action steps you can take?

FOURTEEN

Authenticity—To Move from Playing a Role to Being Your True Self

*I have often thought that the best way to define a person's
character would be to seek out the particular mental or
moral attitude in which, when it came upon them, they felt
themselves most deeply and intensely active and alive. At
such moments there is a voice inside which speaks and says,
"This is the real me!"*

WILLIAM JAMES, 1842–1910

WE BEGIN THIS CHAPTER WITH A story about someone we all know.
We grew up with her. I have selected her not because she always
gets it right—she doesn't—but because she has learned a lesson we all
need to learn.

Bette Midler decided at age fifty-one to abandon her movie career
and return to her roots as a live stage performer. Ironically, this change
took place at the very moment her career had been resurrected by the
box office smash *The First Wives Club*. The question, of course, is why
would she do that?

To understand this remarkable change we must squint our memories
and look back to the place from where she came. Midler began her
career as a New York entertainer, eventually earning her way onto
Broadway. She and her manager then planned a strategy for her to
"move up" to movies because, as Midler said, "Movies seemed like the
natural place to go next. Movies were the top of the line; it was as far as
someone could go."

She had an early hit in *The Rose*, for which she won an Oscar nom-
ination, but spent the next two decades bouncing up and down

between a few modest hits and several duds. After watching a taping of herself on live stage at the age of fifty-one she said, "I've been a fool. I realized that I should have been doing my own stage work all these years. I never should have bought into this movie business. I realized that I have been doing work that didn't require me to use any of my skills.

"They never knew what to do with me. When I tried to [influence the scripts] I was completely trashed as someone who didn't know what she was doing. That was a terrible lesson to learn. I totally disintegrated. I didn't want to get involved anymore. I just wanted to do the job, get paid, and go home.

"I really gypped myself. I did it to myself. It must have been something deep inside me that wanted this so badly that I was willing to put up with all that. As for what that success meant to me, it was very nice. It was a blast. But it meant nothing in the long run."

At fifty-one, Bette Midler has recovered something. She has an excitement about getting back to the thing she loves to do, the thing for which she is uniquely gifted. She said, "Up there [on stage], it's a complete expression of who I am." In other words, "This is the real me!"

Watching that taping of herself on live stage made her realize how deeply she loved that line of work. She realized how much she had to give up to go into movies. She said, "I suppose it's because I got cut down so early that it took me all these years to get back on my feet."[1]

Bette Midler is reinventing herself for the second half of her journey. She is doing this by moving away from playing the "role" she perceived would make her happy.

At her midpoint she realized she had lived out a "role" rather than what's authentic and real. She allowed the mold of her occupation to press her to aim for "the top." She didn't aim for the place that would most allow her to celebrate and showcase her giftedness. Yet, at fifty-one, she is now moving toward finding authenticity in her vocation.

The Problem

The end game of midlife reevaluation is to probe until we find new passion and purpose for the rest of the journey—something authentic.

It is about discovering new meanings for life, new callings, and reinventing yourself.

For the first half of our lives we live out the "role" we perceive will take us where we want to go. Or the "role" someone else prescribed for us. Or the "role" we thought was necessary to make others happy. By midlife, though, we begin to tire of playing a role and long for something deeper, more meaningful—something real. In this chapter we will discuss how to move from living a "role" that pleases others to discovering authenticity.

Not many of us will have the opportunity like Bette Midler to be jolted from a misguided "role" by watching a taped performance of ourselves. Yet, to some extent, we all let the world script us into roles that are inauthentic.

Think how often you set goals to "move up"—not because it's who you are, but because the world says happy is higher. How many of us, too, can say, "I've been a fool. I've been living out a role that others have scripted for me, a role that doesn't celebrate or showcase my talents and gifts. This is not the real me."

How often do you find yourself in a role where your input is not valued? How often do you get beaten down to the point you merely want to do your job, get paid, and go home?

You may have gypped yourself out of ten, twenty, thirty, or more of your productive adult years. What's worse, you know that you did it to yourself. And the success you've achieved? You realize it has meant nothing in the long run.

Ideally, a sense of calling would lead each of us to places where we can celebrate and showcase our unique giftedness. Often, however, we get sidetracked by less satisfying ambitions like fame and fortune—similar to Bette Midler—or power and position, like many others.

Sometimes our culture itself sweeps you into "pro forma" roles that are not "the real you." In *The Sibling Society* author Robert Bly suggests our culture has shifted from requiring us to be good to requiring us to be famous—creating even more pressure to play roles.

Some even end up living the dream a loved one has for them, like the son whose father pushed him to become a doctor. Perhaps the only force stronger than teenage peer pressure is adult peer pressure.

Nothing cripples the human spirit more than the need for approval from others. We end up acting out a role not because that's who we are, but because we know, or think, it will please people.

But now, you long to recover something—the authenticity of your youth that ebbed slowly away when you settled into playing a role. When you awaken in the morning, you want to pulsate with anticipation for the new day. You want to get back to that thing you love to do, that thing you are uniquely gifted to do, that thing that completely expresses who you are. You want to scream at the top of your voice, "This is the real me!"

You can get there from here.

BECOMING STILL

A forty-two-year-old father of three growing kids, ages fifteen, twelve, and ten, wrote me a letter in response to an article I published about ten things men can do to find a success that really counts.

> In my own journey, the first thing I did which really made a difference was something even before trying to do the ten things you mentioned.

> I lost my job in a "restructuring" and, for the first time, began to realize where my real allegiances were. It was really the first time in my life when I sought the Lord honestly.

> I remember sitting in my living room early in the morning with no place to go, but having time to just be with the Lord. I learned for the first time to pray honestly without an agenda, to study the Bible without an agenda, and to listen to God speaking to my heart. This by itself radically changed who I am today.

> You wrote how you stared at your navel for two years. This is it, really. This is the turning point, and the only "task" that can result in inner change. Without something on this order, we might be able to put on a good show. But we are really just being fooled.

You would probably agree that the navel gazing period was the beginning of God's work to build you into the person you are now and are becoming. Maybe what I'm trying to say is men do need ideas about how to be successful, but unless we tell them how to get to know God, it will be like giving a man a luxury car without the key.

I'm convinced that one of the biggest problems today is that people cannot stand the idea of being still. We run like mad so we don't have to stop and think about stuff. In order to truly have a turning point in our lives, we have to learn to be still.

How can we encourage men—even if they don't have a catastrophe—to stop fooling themselves, and to just be honest with God?

Sincerely,
Jack

The faster we go the more shallow we become. The faster a boat goes, the more it rides on top of the water. Speed and depth are opposites. We cannot think deeply about anything when we speed as fast as our stamina will bear across the surface of life.

The inauthentic will find you. You don't have to go in search of it. It beckons you to flash a plastic smile, to laugh a little too hard, to do whatever is necessary to get the deal, and to not waste your time on *that* person.

Authenticity is that which is genuine, true, and real. It takes time and effort to find the authentic. Authenticity is found in deep pools where rivers meander slowly along. It is found next to still ponds, which reward you with reflections if you will look a long while. And it is especially found in the broad lake of midlife.

There is a time to do and there is a time to be. When you suspect you lack authenticity—that you have been playing a role—it is a time to come apart and simply "be" with God.

Two sisters had the extraordinary experience of actually entertaining the historical person of Jesus in their home. One sister, Mary, sat at his feet drinking in his every word. The other sister, Martha, was distracted by unfinished work. Martha asked Jesus to tell her sister to lend a hand. Jesus fascinates us with his response: "'Martha, Martha,' the Lord answered, 'you are worried and upset about many things, but only one thing is needed. Mary has chosen what is better, and it will not be taken away from her'" (Luke 10:41–42).

I'm reminded of Solomon's advice that there is a season for every event under heaven. Mary knew when to simply be. Martha missed her moment. When we are worried and upset by many things perhaps we should take a break. One friend, when he gets stressed out, simply leaves the office and drives to the beach.

THE EXAMINED LIFE

Some of us settle into a repeating seven-, ten-, or twelve-year pattern that starts in humility, builds toward genuine success, derails into pride, accelerates into success out of control, careens into a wall, blows up, finally spewing chaos into our private or public lives or both.

We cannot always advance; sometimes we must retreat. In *The Paradox of Success*,[2] author John O'Neill calls a retreat a "strategic pause." The first step to recover authenticity is to carve out some time to be still, to retreat, to strategically pause, to navel gaze.

By definition, halftime is one of those epochs of life that forces a slow down. You couldn't make your boat go fast enough to plane across the water's surface if you wanted—you simply lack the energy. And the current barely moves you along. You want to regain your authenticity. You find yourself in the right mood for navel gazing.

You've heard people joke about staring at their navels. Though we laugh, many of us don't actually know what that means. What would someone actually do who wanted a profitable time of reflection and self-evaluation?

Each of the remaining chapters in this book is written to help you think through midlife issues in self-examination. In them we will explore a number of practical ideas to find this authenticity of which we've been speaking.

FOCUS QUESTIONS

1. When was the last time you felt deeply and intensely active and alive, wanting to scream, "This is the real me!"? What was it that made you feel that way?

2. What are the "roles" you have played of which you have tired? Did they take you where you wanted to go, and why or why not? Do you feel like you have gypped yourself, and why or why not?

3. In this chapter we raised the issue of moving from playing a "role" that pleases others to discovering a fresh sense of authenticity. Does this resonate with where you are? Describe where you are in that process?

4. If you wanted to cultivate a lifestyle of self-examination, what things would you do? Is this a step you want to take? Explain your answer.

FIFTEEN

Meanings—Identifying New Sources of Meaning

Man's search for meaning is the chief motivation of his life.
VIKTOR FRANKL

J AKE, A MIDDLE MANAGER IN A major company, was hired because of his previous accomplishments and extraordinary gifts. Yet, rather than helping him celebrate his gifts, his new employer increasingly assigns him projects far afield from his gifts, interests, and competencies. It has created deep frustration and confusion.

Ron, on the other hand, hasn't held a position that showcases his gifts for several years. After spending twelve satisfying years with the same company, he has held four different positions in the last six years. He earns less today than he did ten years ago. Understandably, his self-worth and dignity are at a low point. He feels like a failure.

THE PROBLEM

While these two men are at opposite ends of the spectrum in one sense, both are struggling to find meaning in what they do. They are not alone. Many people at their halfway mark are groping for a deeper sense of worth and contribution. They long for a calling that can satisfy their deep desire for value and meaning.

Viktor Frankl said, "Man's search for meaning is the chief motivation of his life." Thoreau said, "The mass of people lead lives of quiet desperation." The sure meaning of Thoreau's statement is that the mass of people have not found Frankl's meaning.

Our most innate need is our need to be significant—to find meaning and purpose. It is the underlying motivator of our behavior. It is what brings us joy, pleasure, peace, and contentment. How many times have you said or felt the following?

- I want my life to count—to make a difference!
- I want to have an impact.
- I want to make a contribution.
- I want to be useful, to do something with my life.
- I want to have a sense of meaning and purpose.

This chapter focuses on helping you identify where you derive your meanings.

THE FOUR CORE SOURCES OF MEANING

God has created us to find meaning—plus the joy and satisfaction that comes with it. Yet, to find God's meaning we must search for God's way. We will find our "meanings" in four core biblical purposes. These four core purposes form the irreducible minimums of the Christian faith. The first two relate to our "tasks," and the second two relate to our "relationships." Let's look briefly at each of them.

1. The Great Commission

Easily the most inspiring, life-changing words ever uttered came from the lips of Jesus. Never have any words so fired people's imaginations. Never have any words mobilized greater armies of good.

"All authority in heaven and on earth has been given to me. Therefore go and make disciples of all nations, baptizing them in the name of the Father and of the Son and of the Holy Spirit, and teaching them to obey everything I have commanded you. And surely I am with you always, to the very end of the age" (Matthew 28:18–20).

During the first half we spend so much of our time establishing, building, advancing, family raising, spouse serving, and scraping to make ends meet. By halftime we often realize that we have missed something. We wish we would have spent more time sharing our faith—helping to bring others along.

One of the exquisite joys of Christian faith is to learn that someone we know has found salvation and meaning through Christ. How much greater the joy when that person is a friend or loved one. Greater still is that joy when we are the ones privileged to introduce them to God. Ironically, our greatest meaning will come from helping others find meaning.

Nothing will put wind in your sails like participating in the Great Commission. If you lack meaning at halftime ask yourself, "Should I make the Great Commission a bigger part of my second half?"

2. The Cultural Commission

As I have said many times, God calls us to build the kingdom and tend the culture. It's not either/or but both/and. While the Great Commission describes the challenge to help build God's kingdom, we tend the culture through the "cultural commission" (Genesis 1:28). This is our calling to make the world a more livable place, to raise families, and to engage in productive work and service.

Your work is not merely a platform for you to serve God—it is serving God. In other words, we don't simply endure work until coffee breaks so we can witness to our coworkers; the work itself is important to God.

What if you can't figure out your calling, or if it seems to have faded on you? A man in his thirties experienced frustration because he couldn't figure out his calling—where he was going. "What am I supposed to do with my life?"

His mentor counseled him, "You don't need to know where you are going. Relax. Let it come to you. It will happen. Simply remain faithful to do what is already before you with excellence. Moses was forty years old when he was called to deliver his people, spent forty years in preparation for his calling and another forty years to execute it. Two thirds of his life had passed before God released him for his ultimate service."

These are encouraging words for someone looking for a second wind.

3. The New Commandment

Jesus did not say, "By this all men will know that you are my disciples, if you perfect your theology." Right theology is important, and bad theology is deadly. Yet, lost and lonely people are not attracted to us by the excellence of our theology (though it should be excellent). People are attracted to us by the way we love one another.

What Jesus did say was, "By this all men will know that you are my disciples, if you love one another" (John 13:35). *The Living Bible* says of love, "All ten [commandments] are wrapped up in this one, to love your neighbor as yourself.... That's why it fully satisfies all of God's requirements. It is the only law you need" (Romans 13:9–10).

In the second-century church, Christians were accused of treason (they wouldn't pledge allegiance to the Roman emperor), cannibalism (drinking the blood of Christ and eating his body), sexual immorality ("the kiss of peace"), and many other things.

Yet, against this backdrop the early church expanded rapidly. God was at work in the way Christians treated each other and loved the unlovely. The church grew on the foundation of love. Julian the Apostate, a pagan, reportedly said, "Those impious Christians. They support not only their own poor, but ours too." It had quite an effect. It still does.

Meaning in the second half will spring from a love for others.

4. The Great Commandment

Jesus said the "greatest" commandment is for us to love God with all of our heart, all of our soul, all of our mind, and all of our strength."

In other words, we are to love God with the totality of our being, the sum of our strength, every ounce of our energy. There is to be an intensity we bring to the loving of God.

Job lost his business empire in a hostile corporate takeover. His children were tragically killed. His health failed. Finally, his wife said, "Why don't you just curse God and die?"

"Oh, foolish woman," he said. Elsewhere, "Though he slay me, yet will I trust in him." Job knew what it meant to love God with the totality of his being.

It is the greatest joy, pleasure, and source of meaning in all of human existence to come humbly to the foot of the cross in full surrender to the lordship of Jesus Christ, who loved us and gave himself as a sacrifice for our sins. It is second wind for the second half.

Every person will find meaning in their own way. However, our meanings should flow from these four universal purposes God has for all people. In fact, everything about Christian life flows from one of these four purposes.

PERSONAL SOURCES OF MEANING

Author James Newman developed a terrific illustration to help us zero in on what's really important. Imagine I invite you to my home for dinner. While we're waiting for the burgers to cook, I take you into the street where a 120-foot-long steel construction beam is lying on the surface. I stand at one end and have you stand at the other. If you walk the distance of the beam, I tell you, I'll give you a thousand dollars. Of course, you leap at the chance.

Now let's change the situation. I truck the I-beam to the World Trade Center—the twin towers in lower Manhattan that loom 1,360 feet above the pavement. At 120 feet the beam stretches just far enough to straddle the two buildings with a foot to spare on each side. It bows slightly at the center, but we bolt it down. It's drizzling and a stiff forty-mile-an-hour wind blows, but what a view!

You stand on one building and I stand on the other. I again offer you a thousand dollars to walk—not crawl—across the beam. Would you still do it? No? How about for ten thousand dollars? ... One hundred thousand? How about one million dollars? You will turn me down, of course. No one in their right mind would take that kind of risk for money.

Let's change the situation again. Suddenly, I turn out to be a monster who has kidnapped your two-year-old grandchild. I'm holding her over the edge of one of the towers by her hair. I tell you, "If you don't get across that beam right now I'm going to drop this kid." Supposing you really believed I was malevolent enough to do it, you would quickly take the risk.

The point, of course, is that very few things would be important enough to attempt crossing the beam.

Conference speaker Hyrum W. Smith was using this illustration once and chose a woman with a teenager to participate in a role play. He had the teenager over the ledge. He told her to come across. She said, "Drop him."

What would be important enough for you to walk across the beam and risk your life? Right now jot down the "few things" important enough to get you out on that beam. These are the deepest sources of personal meaning to us. This exercise quickly shows us how important our lives are to us. Also, we see how few things are more important to us than our lives.

After reading Viktor Frankl's book, *Man's Search for Meaning*, I reflected anew on where my own "meanings" come from.

First, I realized that I do not feel that my life has much meaning unless I have the sense of a vibrant, ongoing personal relationship with Christ (the Great Commandment). Then, out of the overflow of that growing love relationship, I have the desire and energy to share my faith, which also gives me meaning (the Great Commission).

Second, I discovered that to have meaning as a husband I have to feel a strong emotional "connectedness" to my wife, Patsy (the New Commandment). Third, to have meaning as a father I really need to sense that my children are continuing to make progress toward spiritual maturity (the New Commandment).

Finally, it dawned on me that I don't sense meaning as a worker unless I have been able to express my "creativity" and accomplish "productivity" (the Cultural Commission). I tend to produce high volumes of work, and if I'm not careful I can feel "down" at the end of a day that seemed less than fully productive. For me, productivity can range from polishing off my "to do list" to helping a man think through an issue that has him perplexed.

How about you? Do you know where your "meanings" in life come from? In the next chapter, "Setting Priorities—The Passport to a Balanced Second Half," you will have an opportunity to reflect on how you have done in the key areas of your life and think over changes you may want to make. For now, reflect on these questions and feel free to make notes.

FOCUS QUESTIONS

1. In the chapter it was stated, "Our most innate need is our need to be significant—to find meaning and purpose." Do you agree? Why or why not?

2. Viktor Frankl said, "Man's search for meaning is the chief motivation of his life." Thoreau said, "The mass of people lead lives of quiet desperation." The sure meaning of Thoreau's statement is that the mass of people have not found Frankl's meaning. Do you agree with this idea? If so, give an example.

3. Where do your "meanings" come from?

4. Are you happy with your answers to question 3? Do they fairly represent the four core sources of meaning mentioned in this chapter? What would you like to do differently, and how will you do it?

5. Do you derive meanings from your relationships as well as your tasks? Are you "tilted" toward your vocation at the expense of other sources of meaning and purpose? What should you do?

SIXTEEN

Setting Priorities—The Passport to a Balanced Second Half

When you set priorities you are literally writing history in advance.

TOM SKINNER (1942–1994)

ONCE MY WIFE AND I INVITED Holiday Inn cofounder Bill Walton, who experienced a late-in-life conversion, to speak at a dinner party. A Bible study I attend was to meet the following morning so I invited Mr. Walton to go. He was eager to come along.

The next morning a group of about eight men, ages thirty to forty-five, assembled at our table. Each described in two or three minutes where he was on his spiritual pilgrimage.

As each successive man shared, I noticed Mr. Walton becoming more and more fidgety. Finally, it was his turn to speak. He said, "It is true that I helped build one of America's great corporations. But in order to do so I arrived at the office every morning by seven and rarely got home before ten o'clock at night." His brow furrowed, his shoulders drooped, and his lip quivered as he added, "I never saw a single Little League baseball game."

He paused and stared sadly into our faces as though he could see the future. He took a deep breath to gather himself. Then, with trembling fists and booming voice, the room rattled as he roared, "I exhort you, young men. Learn to live by biblical priorities!"

THE PROBLEM

Mr. Walton would have us know that people who fail usually fail because they didn't manage their priorities.

The dictionary says that a "priority" is something to which we give precedence because of its urgency or importance. To "prioritize" means to arrange in order of importance.

Priorities, then, are "pre-decisions," decisions we make to decide in advance what we will give ourselves to. When we set priorities we are literally writing history in advance.

Priorities become a grid to help us distinguish opportunity from distraction. They are filters through which we can sift daily decisions to make sure we keep on track. When we set priorities in advance it reduces the pressure we feel when we must make decisions under fire.

LIVING BY PRIORITIES

Jesus made decisions on the basis of his priorities, not his pressures. One morning after a tiring night of ministry, Jesus went to have some time to himself. It was not to be. . . .

"At daybreak Jesus went out to a solitary place. The people were looking for him and when they came to where he was, they tried to keep him from leaving them. But he said, 'I must preach the good news of the kingdom of God to the other towns also, because that is why I was sent.' And he kept on preaching in the synagogues of Judea" (Luke 4:42–44).

Notice three things. First, the people tried to keep Jesus from leaving. Perhaps they appealed to his compassion for their many needs. The better job you do, the more people will ask you to do. Without intending to, people will ask you to do things that meet their needs, but don't necessarily match your priorities.

Second, Jesus knew his purpose, or calling. He said, "I must preach the good news of the kingdom of God to the other towns also, because that is why I was sent." He let his purpose determine his priorities. He did not let the emotion of the moment cloud his judgment. Since he had decided in advance what he was supposed to do, he was not distracted.

Third, Jesus did what he was called to do. The pressure to do that which is good but not best has put many wagons in the ditch. There is one great rule for priority living we glean from the example of Jesus: Decide what to do on the basis of your priorities not your pressures.

FIVE RULES FOR SETTING PRIORITIES

No man can do everything he wishes. Choices must be made. How can we use priorities to make choices about how we spend and invest our limited time and money during the second half?

First, don't give yourself to those who don't absolutely need you at the expense of those who do. Triage is the military technique of deciding how to prioritize treatment of wounded soldiers when a wave of new casualties swamps the capacity of the medic unit. The helicopters bring back three groups of wounded soldiers:

- Those who will die no matter what is done
- Those who will live even if treatment is delayed
- Those who will live only if given immediate treatment

Can you guess the order of treatment? For our personal decision making we should conduct a little civilian triage:

- Who can't live without you, or you without them?
- Who would it be nice to help if you don't have to neglect the first group?
- Who are those who will be fine with or without you?

Why is it that we often give the most of our time to those who care about us the least, and the least of our time to those who care about us the most? That's why we should decide in advance what our priorities ought to be. That's why we should prioritize everything on the basis of who will cry at our funeral.

Second, distinguish opportunity from distraction. Many times distractions come disguised as opportunities. Unless we have thought through who we are, what our lives are all about, and what's important to us, we will not have the focus to choose the best. Author and marketing strategist Al Ries says that focus is the art of exclusion. A great secret of priority living is to have so thought through your life that deciding what to include and exclude becomes second nature.

Third, never do anything someone else can do. Many years ago I decided that I would only do things I do well. That served a good purpose, because it kept me in my areas of competence. However, I have also realized that simply because I can do something well doesn't mean it's the best use of my time.

Since then I've added a "part two." I also don't do anything if someone else can also do it. Since I write and prepare messages at my home office, this means if I need a copy I get up and make it at my copy machine. When I'm at the office I have someone else make the copy. However, if no one is available, I make it. This frees up an unusually large amount of time. Why not give it a try? (But don't tell your wife to take out the trash. It really is something only you can do—for reasons that should be obvious!)

Fourth, plan to neglect that which doesn't move you closer to your goal. A young woman became a virtuoso violinist. When asked the secret of her success, she told a fascinating story. When she was a child she would come home from school, have a snack, play with her friends, do her chores and homework, and then she would practice her violin. As you might expect, many days she simply ran out of time.

Then one day she set her mind on moving to the next level. She began to exercise what she termed "planned neglect." With this new idea, when she came home from school she gave practice the first priority. She planned to neglect everything that didn't move her closer to her goal. Only when she finished practice would she do other things. "Planned neglect" is a great lesson for anyone who has had trouble finding time to do the thing they really would like to do.

Fifth, recognize the difference between a good idea and a God idea.[1] We are naturally inclined to act on the impulse of a good idea. Not every good idea is from God. Sometimes good ideas get in the way of God ideas. Peter wanted to build three shelters for Moses, Elijah, and Jesus at the Transfiguration. The Bible says, "While he was still speaking, a bright cloud enveloped them" (Matthew 17:5). In other words, Peter's good idea was so impetuous that God literally interrupted Peter—"while he was still speaking."

Prayer removes the impulse of the good idea, the good idea born of human ingenuity but not of God. Pray first, then make your plan. It is the habit of someone who would distinguish between good and God.

AREAS TO PRIORITIZE

In the second half we will have much more freedom to choose our own priorities. So much of the first half was scripted for us by our obligations and the roles we accepted.

The second half is going to be radically different. You will have two things in the second half that were in scarce supply in the first half: time and money. The key to success in the second half is to "spend" your discretionary time and money by prayerfully God-shaped priorities. It's to decide in advance—now—what really matters to you because God lives in you, and then how you will live as a result. What are the areas that we will prioritize?

Every person must take personal responsibility for their lives in eight areas:

- relationship with God
- relationship with your spouse (if married)
- relationship with your children and grandchildren (if applicable)
- friendships
- finances
- health (including leisure, exercise, and rest)
- work
- personal ministry

How much of a priority has each of these areas been to you? What changes will you make? What will you invest (and give up) to realize these changes?

LIFE TASKS

During the first half our priorities, and therefore our life tasks, revolved around establishing ourselves, accumulating, and parenting. Dramatic changes in the way we think start to occur in the second half. For example, financially we shift from accumulation to preservation. We shift from taking care of children to taking care of aging parents.

The three major life tasks for which midlifers must prepare are retirement, health, and aging parents. The purpose of this section is to surface these issues, not necessarily to offer suggestions in dealing with them. I trust the visibility will trigger your thinking in the days ahead.

1. *Retirement.* The first issue of retirement is whether or not to retire. Increasingly, good health and financial need are leading people to not retire. If you do retire it is often said, "Better to retire to something than from something." Will you downsize your home? Where will you live? What will you do? Will your finances allow you to do what you wish?

2. *Health.* The baby boom lasted from 1946 to 1964, during which roughly seventy-five million children were born. If you were born during those years your average life expectancy if male is about seventy-seven years and if female about eighty-two years (slightly less if African American).[2]

Of course, tragedies cut some lives short unexpectedly. However, we can influence the length and quality of our lives by living responsibly and treating our bodies as "the temple of the Holy Spirit." Here are some questions to consider: Do you have eating habits that will prolong life? Do you take exercise sufficient for good health? Do you get enough sleep? Are you under too much stress for good health? Do you have athletic and/or hobby interests for recreation? Do you regularly have a physical examination? Do you have an adequate insurance program for major medical, nursing care, and disability?

3. *Aging Parents.* About the time we finally marry off our kids and end the child-care phase we roll right into the parent-care phase. With people living longer, no life task looms larger than taking care of our parents as they age. What thoughts or plans do you and your siblings, if any, have if the health of one or both or your parents should fail? What if they cannot make it financially? How will you handle that? Are there unresolved relationship issues? How will you make decisions about nursing care versus remaining in their own home or moving in with you or a sibling? Who will handle funeral and probate responsibilities? Have you made sure you have no "unfinished business" with your parents?

Focus Questions

1. To what degree has living by priorities been a part of your life? If significant, what has been the main advantage? If not much, what do you think you may have lost?

2. Have you given yourself to those who don't need you at the expense of those who do? If yes, look back at the "civilian triage" idea and consider how this can help you in the second half.
3. How can setting priorities help you distinguish opportunity from distraction in the future?
4. How can the principle of "planned neglect" help you find the authenticity we all seek?
5. Eight areas to prioritize were mentioned in this chapter. Which one of these has been your strongest area and why? Which one has been your weakest area, and what would you like to do about it?
6. Which of the three life tasks mentioned—retirement, health, and aging parents—have you begun to think about? What would be one next step to take for each?

SEVENTEEN

A Cause to Champion—Writing a Life Mission Statement

The best time to plant a tree was twenty years ago.
The second best time is now.

CHINESE PROVERB

IN THE MOVIE *JERRY MAGUIRE*, TOM Cruise plays the role of a thirty-five-year-old sports agent in an early midlife career crisis.

Jerry Maguire reigned as the top agent in the hyper-competitive world of professional sports. Yet, the duplicity of how he did his job began to gnaw away at him. One night at a corporate conference he couldn't sleep. Jerry said in the voice over, "I couldn't escape one simple thought. I hated myself. No, no, no, here's what it was. . . . I hated my place in the world."

He began to write a mission statement, a suggestion for the future of the company for which he worked. He stayed up all night. As he wrote he said, "Suddenly, I was my father's son again. I was remembering the simple pleasures of this job. How I ended up here out of law school. The way a stadium sounds when one of my players performs well. The way we are meant to protect them in health and injuries. With so many clients, we had forgotten what was important."

He wrote and wrote and wrote. Suddenly, everything became clear to him. The answer for him was fewer clients, more attention, caring for the clients, caring for himself. He said, "It was the me I had always wanted to be. I was thirty-five. I had started my life."

THE PROBLEM

We all have low points when we hate our place in the world. It is during these times that we long to remember the simple pleasures and what's important. When we spiral down so far that we hate our place in

165

the world, how do we recapture passion for life? How do you and I get back to being the "me I always wanted to be"? What will it take for everything to "become clear"?

During the parenthesis between the first and second half our consuming desire is to find a mission or task so engaging that we will occasionally feel compelled to let out an involuntary "whoop!" (Remember how good that feels?) We need a cause to champion. By the time we arrive at midpoint, however, the pressure of pursuing first-half success has often choked the whoop right out of us!

In the last four chapters we have seen that success in the second half depends on settling the "who you are" issues—attitudes, authenticity, the examined life, meanings, priorities, and values. Success in the second half likewise depends on settling the "what you do" issues—life purpose, calling, vision, and mission.

In this chapter I want to walk you through a "method" or "process" for making things clear for the second half. It's only one way, but perhaps you will find it valuable. The goal is to equip you to write or rewrite a Life Mission Statement. It's a process by which you can clarify the new dream, cause, or task you've been thinking about.

I don't get too hung up on "technique," and I don't want you to either. There is no one right way to probe for the "cause" God has for your life. This can be as hard or soft, as long-term or short-term, as focused or generalized as you want. I realize this approach goes against the grain of getting really specific, but I want us to think biblically rather than Western. Generally, the areas to cover in a Life Mission Statement can include, but need not be limited to, the following subjects which we will flesh out directly:

- A life purpose—why you exist
- A calling—what you do
- A vision—a mental picture of what you want to happen
- A mission—how you will go about it

FIRST-HALF AUDIT

In business planning it's understood that you can't determine where you want to go until you know where you are. This assessment is often called "the current situation." So, the first step in developing a new Life Mission Statement is to make sure you understand where you are—your "current situation."

Now I'd like you to get started by reflecting on "your life so far." It's a sort of first-half audit. Since writing makes a more precise person, it is doubly good to write this understanding on paper. You can write anything you want—as detailed or general as you wish. However, here are the types of things I would like you to reflect on as you paint with words the portrait of your life so far:

- Your overall satisfaction
- Milestones
- Major goals, met and unmet
- Significant achievements and satisfying results
- Priorities, right and wrong
- Failures and lessons learned
- Regrets and things you want to improve
- Met and unmet dreams
- Fears, doubts, pressures, and concerns about the past, present, and future

Be balanced. Don't beat yourself up. Be humble, but don't sell yourself short. Use the 80/20 rule—eighty percent of the space for positive reflections and twenty percent for improvement areas. Use as much imagination as you want, or you can follow the flow of the guideline above. Okay, it's time to go to work. On paper or on your computer, assess the current situation of your life.

LIFE MISSION STATEMENT

In the same way Jerry Maguire wrote a suggestion for the future of his company, I want to equip you to write a suggestion for the future of your life. We will call it a Life Mission Statement. Let's develop each of the four pieces already mentioned. The first is "life purpose."

A Life Purpose—Why You Exist

A life purpose can cover any time horizon, but it's generally long term—ten years or more. It reflects your understanding of what God wants you to give your life to at both the highest and the most basic levels. It is both the first reason and the ultimate reason you draw breath. It may focus on "being" or "doing" or both. From my perspective, though, I don't think we can do what God wants us to "do" until we become what God wants us to "be." For that reason I would generally say your life purpose should first reflect the kind of person you want to become and then, if you like, what you want to do.

My own life purpose is "to live the rest of my earthly life for the will of God." This certainly zeroes in on "doing," but notice that I cannot "do" anything until I know the will of God. And I can't know the will of God unless I spend time with him in solitude, study, and reflection. So while my life purpose may seem "doing" oriented, it also loops in a number of other more reflective ideas.

Recently I developed a "focusing" idea for myself (a sort of "second" life purpose): No agenda but God; no agenda but God's. I think this captures two important ideas about our life purpose. First, our purpose must fit into the larger context of what God is doing. Second, there is a balance between being and doing.

Here are several thoughts I have previously written about life purpose:

The idea of a life purpose answers life's larger questions—not what do I do today, but "Why do I exist? What are my functions in life?" It reflects our examination of life's larger meaning. Our life purpose is what God wants us to do long-term, it's why he put us here. A life purpose is the thread of continuity that you can weave into the long-term view of your life. It relates to how you perceive the theory of your life.

The getting of this life purpose statement can be the hardest kind of work, exacting and exhausting, but well worth the effort. Once settled, it is a constant reminder of why you exist. It describes in a general and overarching way what your life is all about. Like a compass, it points the way to the meaning and significance we all yearn for. Like a gyroscope, whenever you are knocked off balance it will help you stand upright. It answers the questions "Why do I exist?" and "What is the purpose of my life?"[1]

What was your Life Purpose for the first half? Do you know yet what God's Life Purpose is for your second half? If so, I'm going to ask you to write it down on the "Life Mission Statement" worksheet at the end of this chapter. If you aren't sure about your Life Purpose for the second half, here are a few steps to take:

1.*Ask God to reveal your Life Purpose to you.* Read Psalm 32:8 and trust in God's promise that he will answer.

2.*Search the Scriptures for verses and phrases that capture your sense of God's purpose for your earthly life.* Look for verses that describe your area of passion. Record verses that give you a special sense of meaning and purpose, picking out themes that are big enough to last a lifetime. Here are some to get you started: Joshua 24:15; Proverbs 3:5–6; Matthew 6:33; Matthew 22:37–40; Matthew 28:19–20; John 4:34; John 15:1–9, 15; John 17:4; Acts 20:24; 1 Corinthians 10:31; Ephesians 2:10; Philippians 3:10; Proverbs 30:7–9; Micah 6:8; Acts 1:8; Ecclesiastes 12:13.

3.*Go slowly and wait for God to reveal himself.* Be patient; it may take some time. It may take weeks or months.

4.*Once you find the verses and phrases that you believe express your Life Purpose, create a concise summary statement.* Write a "draft" statement.

Once you are satisfied with it, write it down on the "Life Mission Statement" worksheet at the end of this chapter and in the front of your Bible, and date it.

A Calling—What You Give Yourself To

In addition to settling the issue of life purpose—"why you exist," you must also settle the important question of calling—"what you will do." Are not questions about our life purpose and calling what truly define the midlife experience?

What is a "calling"? Here's a good working definition: A calling is that vocation to which you can give yourself unreservedly and which arouses a passionate desire for excellence. It is the thing you are "able" to do because of interest, gifting, and capability. It may be for a wage but not necessarily. It may be in the ministry but not usually. It can be as formal as a job or as informal as "what you do during the day."

It is probably not as tightly defined as a specific "job description" you do or a company you work for, but the "type" of work you can give yourself to with enthusiasm. Examples of calling could include sales work, management, engineering, the practice of law, or plumbing. Or you may choose to describe your calling at the level of your "life's work" and remain more general, describing it in terms of "solving problems" rather than management, or "designing things" instead of engineering.

President Eisenhower once said, "We succeed only as we identify in life, or in war, or in anything else, a single overriding objective, and make all other considerations bend to that one objective."

Picture two people working at the same job, say ticket agents for an airline. To one his work is merely a job—something he does for eight hours daily to get money so he can do the things he really wants to do. He finds no particular joy in his work. He rarely feels a squirt of adrenaline or finds satisfaction in helping someone with a special problem. In fact, people with special needs irritate him.

The second ticket agent performs the exact same tasks as the first. However, this agent believes his calling is "to serve travelers." He senses his "life's work" is to serve others. He gets out of bed looking forward to his day. Sure, he has difficult customers, but he shrugs off his bad experiences.

He sees his work as a cause—part of a worldwide network of transportation that connects people to their distant families, enables families to vacation together for renewal, and keeps the wheels of commerce greased. He knows he belongs to something larger than himself and that it is noble, wholesome, and worthwhile.

His calling is not to a specific job or a specific company, but to a "life work" of serving others. He could be equally motivated by any number of other jobs, as long as he could enjoy the satisfaction of serving others for a cause in which he believes—like auto sales, customer service, or hospital admitting. On the other hand, he may feel particularly called to the travel industry by interest.

As you can see, a calling includes what you do, but it is more. It is something you can give yourself to for the betterment of humankind, which at the same time brings you joy and fulfillment. It is the vocation that kindles fresh fire each new morning. A calling is not merely a means to other ends (though it will be); a calling is an end in itself.

Michael Novak, in his book *Business As a Calling*, says a true calling reveals its presence by the enjoyment and sense of renewed energies we gain when we do it. It's not that we don't dread difficult tasks (we do) but, knowing it is part of our duty, we soldier on. In fact, there is an odd satisfaction in the ability to bear certain kinds of pain. Novak goes on to make the point that callings are not usually easy to discover.[2]

Callings are particularly difficult to revamp or rejuvenate at midlife. Why is that? Assuming you had a true calling during your first half, let's suppose you've gotten pretty good at what you do. Your calling was good to you. Perhaps you still love what you do, or maybe you've lost interest. In either case, now you wonder, *Is this what I really want to give myself to for the rest of my career or life?* It's an appropriate question.

Maybe you've exceeded your expectations and want a new challenge. Can this desire be satisfied where you are? Or maybe you have not lived up to your own expectations and can't figure out why. Is it your attitude? Is it your technical ability? Is it your ability to get along with people? Is it a matter of talent or getting the right break? All of these questions loom larger at midlife because the end of the runway is in sight. You may even feel like time is running out (it isn't).

No task of the midlife experience is more all-consuming than discovering a new, or reaffirming an old, calling. Recently a thirty-nine-year-old man looking for a new calling told me that his life's work is "organizing things" and that he is motivated by "a cause." This understanding of himself gives him two exceptional clues to find his new calling.

Here are some questions that may give you some additional clues about your calling.

- What are your natural abilities?
- What are your unique gifts?
- What special competency do you have?
- What are you trained to do?
- Do you consider your training valuable for your interests?

- What types of "tasks" interest you? (e.g., innovating, designing, developing, organizing, planning, controlling, directing, persuading, mentoring)
- What types of "jobs" or "work" interest you? (e.g., accounting, engineering)

What was your calling for the first half? Do you know yet what God's calling is for your second half? If so, go ahead and write it down on your copy of the Life Mission Statement worksheet that follows the Focus Questions at the end of the chapter. If you don't know your second-half calling here are twelve suggestions to help you discover it, reproduced from my book *The Seven Seasons of a Man's Life*. Look these over and be patient. Personally, from the time I began to "tire" of my calling to real estate until I changed vocations was six years. Even then, it was an "unclear" calling for another four years—that's ten years altogether. Admittedly, my experience was on the long side, but it happens.

Twelve Suggestions

1. *Employ the means of guidance.* To help us discern his will, God has given seven means of guidance: the Bible, prayer, the Holy Spirit, our conscience, our circumstances, counsel, and fasting. Use these with liberality, keeping before you the question "God, what is Your calling for my life?"

2. *Discover your spiritual gifts.* Make the effort to learn your spiritual gifts. This will help you discern your direction as much as any single thing. Your church may offer training in spiritual gifts. Ask your pastor. Also, check with your local Christian bookstore for books and other resources. If you have a Bible study leader, ask him to help you. Knowing your gifts will help you in your work as well in a personal ministry. For example, a person with the gifts of leadership and faith may be suited to own his own business.

3. *Identify your motivated interests.* Philippians 2:13 says, "For it is God who works in you to will and to act according to his good purpose." In other words, God puts desires into our hearts to do his work. Pay attention to your desires. Pray over them and see if your motives are pure.

Getting in touch with your motivated interests can help you direct career choices as well as choose personal ministry opportunities.

4. *Complete your written Life Purpose Statement.* To understand God's larger purpose for your life is to know why you are here and what your life is about. Develop a written Life Purpose Statement of one or two sentences. Base it on a Scripture verse if possible.

5. *Keep a journal.* Consider keeping a written journal of Bible verses that touch you, impressions you have, your concerns, new insights about yourself, the character of God, and his calling. Look for patterns of interest or concern.

6. *Keep driving toward the vision.* Vision is a mental picture of a desirable future. Eventually, God will give you a picture of what he wants you to do. This may be more or less clear. An old country preacher said, "Clarity of vision means an acceleration toward the goal." When early-morning fog reduces our vision we must drive more slowly. But when the fog burns off we can speed up. We all go through periods when we know where we want to go, but the way to get there seems fogged up. The key is to always keep driving toward the vision, even if you must drive slowly because you are in a fog. Act in light of what you do know. Don't not act in light of what you don't know.

7. *Pray about what to do when strategy is unclear.* When how God wants us to undertake our vision is unclear, we must pray and wait patiently. These are the times when he is equipping us—preparing us—with all we will need to successfully fulfill the vision. It may be his will to keep things unclear for forty years, as in the case of Moses. Keep moving with what you've seen so far, while praying for what you still need to see.

8. *Reorganize work life to allow for personal ministry.* Jim refused a promotion because it would put him on the road four days a week. Linn quit a position because his boss wanted him to work seven days a week. He found a job selling light bulbs with 1,325 established accounts that required a normal forty-hour week. Don't be so bogged down in work that you never have time to serve the Lord in other ministry capacities besides your work.

9. *Employ the power of faith.* After winning the U. S. Open and Wimbledon, number-one ranked tennis pro, Pete Sampras, was asked if he thought he could win the Grand Slam (the four major international

tennis tournaments) like his hero Rod Laver did in 1968. No one since Laver has won it.

He answered, "No." That pretty well sealed his fate. The negative power of disbelief will cripple your vision. But the power of belief or faith is enormous. Faith is not mere positive thinking; faith is believing God in the face of unbelievable circumstances. It is trusting that what God puts in your heart as "desire" is within his power to bring about.

10. *Maintain priorities.* Regardless of what specific ministry or occupation God gives us, we all have inescapable priorities that we must not neglect. For example, our spouses and children (if applicable), our walk with Christ, personal finances, rest, exercise, and work. We must take responsibility for our own private lives.

11. *Expect opposition.* Live your life in light of the vision God has given you. Don't let opposition deter you. God gave Nehemiah a vision to rebuild his city, but Nehemiah encountered stiff opposition. Nehemiah 4:9 says, "We prayed to our God and posted a guard day and night to meet this threat." In other words, praise the Lord and pass the ammunition! In the end, God fulfilled the vision he put in Nehemiah's heart, a vision that at one point appeared dead.

12. *Be willing to take some risks.* After an invigorating discussion on calling, equipping, and sending, a man said with tears in his eyes, "But I'm just not feeling called." The counsel to this man, who at the time was not serving the Lord at all, was, "Do *something*." Many men never attempt anything significant because they might fail. They would rather be perfect in potentiality than imperfect in actuality.

A Vision—What You Want to Accomplish

If you find yourself in a midlife "funk," it may be that what you need is not a new calling but a new vision.

One man found himself in such a funk in his late forties. He questioned if he was where God wanted him to be. He had earned a Ph.D., held a prestigious position as a university professor, and led a satisfying life. He was truly grateful for his blessings, but he wanted "more." He was considering whether or not to leave his secure position as a professor.

Actually, what this man needed was not a new calling, but a new challenge (or dream or vision). He was well suited by interest, aptitude, and training to be a university professor. The problem was that he had already achieved all of his goals. He had nothing left to accomplish or prove to himself or others. Of course, there are always other dreams to dream, and this is the task he must now give himself to—finding a new vision.

A new vision must spring up from a foundation of gratitude for what God has already done to use us and make us useful. The motivation cannot merely be wanderlust; not more for the sake of more. Rather, one chapter has closed and another beckons to be opened.

If *life purpose* describes in a general way why you exist, and if *calling* is the vocation you give yourself to that arouses passion, then a *vision* describes in a "specific" way what you dream of accomplishing. Think of it this way: calling is *what you do*, purpose is *why you do it*, and vision is *what will happen as a result*. Obviously, there is a lot of overlap.

Leadership authors Bennis and Nanus say that vision is a "mental image of a possible and desirable future state."[3] The Bible says, "Where there is no vision, the people perish" (Proverbs 29:18 KJV). This word *vision* literally means "a mental sight," and can be translated as "dream" or "revelation," in addition to "vision." So, a vision is a "mental picture" you draw in your mind of the future you want to happen. And when people don't have a vision or mental picture they "perish"—which is to say things don't work out. *The Message* paraphrase of the Bible puts it this way: "If people can't see what God is doing, they stumble all over themselves."

A vision is a goal—a big one. Visions are not the work of today or tomorrow or even next month. Rather, a vision has a longer term.

Visions rarely turn out exactly as planned. The apostle Paul had the vision of going to Jerusalem and then on to Rome. I'm sure he didn't consider that he would make those visits as a prisoner, but that's how it came about.

God is the architect of purpose, calling, and vision. He gives us reason to exist, a calling to occupy ourselves, and new visions to pursue. He puts desires in our hearts and then, when we are ready, he gives us those desires.

Often, God must delay the fulfilling of a vision or desire until he has prepared us to be people who can handle it with grace and humility. It is not the nature of God to give us greater visions and accomplishments if they will work to our destruction. Instead, God allows us to be hammered into the shape of a vessel that can gracefully contain the vision. Enter the midlife funk. Much of midlife's pain comes from absorbing the blows that shape our future—a future that is good.

What was your vision for the first half? Do you know yet what God's vision is for your second half? If you do know, please write it down on the Life Mission Statement worksheet at the end of the chapter. If you don't know your second-half vision yet, consider these questions:

- Have you heard a sermon or speech recently that challenged you?
- Is there a specific goal that ignites your imagination?
- Is there something you would love to tackle but have been afraid you would fail?
- What would you like to accomplish if there were no obstacles?
- Do you see a need in the world that you would love to pour yourself into as God's representative?
- Is there one thing you could focus your energy on that would yield a bigger return than spreading yourself in several areas?
- What would you like to be remembered for? (This can be as broad or narrow as you wish).
- How would you describe the picture of the perfect finish to your life?

A Mission—How You Will Go About It

After you have thought through and settled your life purpose and calling and have a vision, you have the final step of describing the "particulars" of how you will go about it—your mission. Your mission is a plan for how you will get where you want to go, what you will do, and (if you like detail) the specific steps and activities you will undertake.

For example, my vocational vision is to help bring about a spiritual awakening by reaching every man in America with a compelling opportunity to be transformed by Jesus Christ. It is the mental picture of what I would like to see happen. This vision is not difficult, it's impossible. Frankly, I some-times think I would gladly settle for something much smaller (and more realistic). But when I think in that direction the fire that burns within me begins to smolder. Anything less doesn't turn my crank.

My vision gives birth to my mission. My vision "suggests" the strategies we can try out to achieve the vision. For example, the only way this vision could be accomplished would be for the whole church (350,000+ individual churches) to focus on reaching men. So, that begins another thought process. How do we connect with denominations? How do we connect with other men's ministries? How can we help the local pastor reach his men?

As a response to all of this, my mission includes the specifics (or strategies) of helping form the National Coalition of Men's Ministries, helping pastors reach men on the fringe of their churches and develop-ing new strategies of evangelism and discipleship. God has made no promise of success, but he has called me to try. Who knows? It may be that dozens of organizations with similar dreams end up working together to accomplish what none of us could do alone.

Also, as I mentioned in chapter 15, in my personal life my "mean-ings" come from sensing vibrancy in my relationship with Christ, con-nectedness with my wife, and spiritual progress in our children. In addition, in chapter 16, I mentioned priorities and life tasks that I, as you, must also factor. Combined, these all suggest particular goals, strategies, and plans—a mission—to make these become reality.

A friend has as his vision—*what* he wants to accomplish—to be a faithful husband, father, churchman, and businessman as a steward of what God has entrusted to him. His mission—*how* he plans to accom-plish it—is to live by biblical priorities, be home for dinner every night, not miss any of his kids ball games and events except for emergencies, spend twenty minutes in meaningful conversation with his wife most days, take her out on a weekly date, view his vocation as a calling from God, and contribute five hours a week to minister to others through his church. He actively shares his faith through an evangelism program in his church. He and his wife desire to take early retirement when he reaches fifty-five to work with underprivileged children.

How about you? What are the strategies, goals, and plans suggested by your vision? Can you describe your mission yet? If so, go ahead and write it down on the Life Mission Statement worksheet.

WRITING A LIFE MISSION STATEMENT

In this chapter we have looked at

- Life purpose—why you exist, generally, why you do what you do
- Calling—what you do, specifically, the thing you do that arouses passion
- Vision—what you want to accomplish, the big picture, the desired future that enflames your imagination
- Mission—how you accomplish it, the particulars, the strategies, goals, and plans to reach your vision

Obviously, there are no hard and fast boundaries between these ideas. All together they weave together into a single cloth of our Life Mission.

If you have not already done so, in the space provided take a first pass at a Life Mission Statement for your second half. Write to the best of your present understanding. If you need to leave something blank, no problem. If you want to take some time to think it over and come back to it, no problem. Do it, and you will be able to say, "It's the authentic me I've always wanted to be. This is a cause that will make me whoop again. I feel good about entering the second half."

LIFE MISSION STATEMENT

My Life Purpose

_____

_____

_____

_____

_____

My Calling

_____

_____

_____

_____

_____

My Vision

_____
_____
_____
_____
_____
_____
_____

My Mission

_____
_____
_____
_____
_____
_____
_____

FOCUS QUESTIONS

1. Has there been a time in your life when you could say, "I'm the authentic me I always wanted to be"? What was it about that season that enabled you to feel that way? Do you feel that way now, and why or why not?

2. When is the last time you let out a whoop? Have you been in the funk that makes you wonder if you will every whoop again? How has this book been helping you to clarify and refocus for the second half? Can you see "whooping" in your immediate future? Why or why not?

3. Were you surprised by anything you wrote down in your "First-Half Audit"? What fresh perspectives on your life did you gain? Have you been guilty of beating yourself up too much?

4. This chapter focused on the "what you do" issues—life purpose, calling, vision, and mission. How clear are you right now about each of these, and why? Take them one by one.

5. Did you complete writing a Life Mission Statement for the second half? If not, will you? How does this give you second wind?

EIGHTEEN

Walking with God—Cultivating a Hunger for the God Who Is

I have treated many hundreds of patients. Among those over thirty-five, there has not been one whose problem in the last resort was not that of finding a religious outlook on life.

CARL JUNG

AUTHOR KEN MYERS TELLS AN INTERESTING story. In college he got into the habit of grabbing a cardboard cup of instant coffee from a machine on the way to his first class. His interest, of course, was jump-starting his brain, not indulging his taste buds.

Several weeks later a friend offered him a cup of freshly ground, freshly brewed, real coffee. Finding it no kin to the thin, bitter liquid to which he had become accustomed, he didn't care for it. For a long time after that he actually preferred the cardboard coffee. Only after he had weaned himself off the instant did he come to appreciate the real thing.[1]

THE PROBLEM

In many ways this story sums up what can happen to us. We so order things that we often live in what we might call a "structural hurry." The pace required to keep up with our "structured" obligations can lead us into a convenient-but-cardboard lifestyle. One man even feels he has to speed to and from work to "save time."

This structural hurry finds its way into our religion. If we're not careful, we can find ourselves drinking a convenient-but-watered-down religion. By midlife, however, our spiritual digestion system begins to rebel. We realize that "hurried" religion tastes thin, bitter. We long for the real God. There are no shortcuts to God. If we want to reconnect with God we will have to "do time" with him.

One of the most frequent concerns I hear is, "I don't sense the presence of God in my life right now." Indeed, I often feel that way myself.

SOLUTIONS

How can you and I gain a greater sense of standing in the presence of the Lord?

First, do what you must to bring yourself consciously into the presence of God. (He's always there.) If you want to feel closer to your husband or wife, you don't get there by dwelling on yourself. It's the same with God.

Second, expand your knowledge and concept of God. Personally, I am always on the lookout for a book that can show me the nature and character of God in a more revealing way. Check with your pastor or a Christian bookstore.

Third, identify which spiritual activities and disciplines appeal most to how you are wired. My twenty-two-year-old daughter was involved with a ministry that stresses "TAWG"—"time alone with God." We don't need to be ritualistic, dogmatic, or legalistic about spending time with God, but we do need to do it.

THE MOMENT OF HUMILITY

One idea to "sense the presence of God" is to set aside some time each day to be with him until you experience "the moment of humility." Every seeker of true communion and worship should thirst each day for a moment of humility with God. The moment of humility is an instant of personal, existential experience with the living Lord. It is pressing, pleading, and pining for the personal reality of God to be manifest in your life.

This moment comes from considering two things: our own mortality and the awesome nature of God—and more so the latter. We contemplate God through prayer, Bible reading, singing, journaling our thoughts, or meditating on the wonders of creation. We say, "I will not yield to any ordinary day. I will stay with God until by contemplating him I am struck with a moment of awe, of transcendence, of being over-whelmed, of sensing a deep gratitude, of desire to praise and worship."

This moment is an instant of clarity. The heavens open for a brief moment, and we see God in a larger way. Then the veil closes back, but we have changed. It is a moment of insight. It is a gaze at the beauty of his holiness; a glimpse of the perfection of his beauty. And then it is gone. But the fading memory of it clings to us until tomorrow when, again, we come to him seeking once more to be humbled in a moment by his greatness, his goodness, and his love.

A moment of humility may come upon us as an overwhelming "heav-iness," a spine-tingling insight into a passage of Scripture, a godly sor-row at seeing the "gravity" of our own sinfulness, feeling the weight of God's love, a warm embrace by the Holy Spirit, the release of bitterness, the joy of forgiving someone who has hurt us. You may experience the moment of humility by staring into the evening sky, by looking at a pic-ture of your children, by recalling how much your spouse has blessed you, or remembering how God has provided. You may weep or feel a squirt of adrenaline.

Let me give an example. One day I experienced the moment of humility while twisting my brain over what every child has pondered: gravity. In the early hour before dawn I was in my backyard gazing into a dark sky filled with little pebbles of diamond fire. I was sitting in a favorite chair perched atop a huge globe twenty-five thousand miles in circumference spinning at a thousand miles per hour. Though traveling a thousand miles per hour, if you jump up you land in the same place. Why is that? If a plane travels with the spin of the earth at five hundred miles per hour, why doesn't the plane go fifteen hundred miles per hour, or does it? Or, if the plane goes against the earth's rotation, why doesn't the plane go backwards five hundred miles per hour, or does it? Or, if you hovered in a helicopter, why doesn't the earth disappear beneath you at a thousand miles per hour? The effect on me was simple. Notwith-standing Einstein's explanation, I broke out in exultation and praise to God for the mysteries and excellencies of his creation. It was, for me, the moment of humility that released me to the rest of my day.

Let me give another example. Recently, I was sitting in our backyard before dawn, gazing into a sky arrayed with countless blinking stars, seeking a greater sense of God's presence in my life. He seemed far, far away.

I concentrated on casting all earthly distractions and cares at the foot of the cross. I tried to quiet myself, thinking of the psalmist: "Be still, and know that I am God" (Psalm 46:10). As I contemplated the twinkling lights I was reminded of that child's query, "Twinkle, twinkle little star, how I wonder what you are."

Soon I turned my attention to my immediate surroundings. The sleeping lawn chairs, the napping picnic table, the snoring trees, and the grass soaked in early morning dew all seemed somehow more "present."

My mind swirled at the thought that right there in front of me, in a silent cube of space that I marked off with my hands, were all of the day's news and sounds in radio, television, cellular, and microwaves. I was reminded that the Holy Spirit of God, too, was in that space. He is omnipresent.

Then, after forty-five minutes or so, it happened. I could "sense" the presence of God. It was not as though God came suddenly. No, it was clear that he had been there all along. Rather, it was I who had suddenly become conscious of his presence.

Personally, I have come to a point in my life that I am not willing to leave my quiet place until that moment of humility has come each day. I find that "moment" is the thing that fills me to overflow in my relationship with Christ. It is a spiritual feast. It is an encounter with the God who is.

In the middle of the midlife lake, when things have slowed down for the season, no activity we undertake will be of more benefit than to cultivate a fresh hunger for God, to seek his presence, and to come to know him as he is.

EIGHT PRACTICAL IDEAS

Each of us is wired to sense God in many ways. You will no doubt relate to each of the following suggestions. On the other hand, you will especially identify with some. As you read along, make a mental note of the ideas that most appeal to you. Then pick one or two practical suggestions to try out.

1. *Contemplation.* Some people are contemplative. They experience a greater awareness of God when they think about who he is and what he has done. There are two ways to contemplate God: in his works (general revelation, nature) and in his Word (special revelation, the Bible).

Suggested Application: Sit quietly in a quiet room at a quiet time of the day. Become aware of everything in the room—the noises, the silence, the creaks, the wind or lack of it, the humidity, the temperature, your body, the furniture, the light, each chair, fabric, texture, color, and how these things make you feel. Consider what else is in the room that you cannot see—radio waves, TV waves, microwaves, cellular phone conversations, HAM radio transmissions. Become aware of the Spirit of God in the room, in the same sense that he was always there even when you were not focused on him. Pray, "Jesus, I know that you are right here with me. [As appropriate] I do sense your presence."

2. *Beauty.* God has made us to appreciate beauty. For some people, a blazing sunset or majestic, haze-covered mountain will bring them into the conscious presence of God.

Suggested Applications:

- Sit quietly in the predawn hour gazing into the sky.
- Watch a vermilion sky yield to a new day or to darkness.
- Go sit still beside a stream.
- Watch an ant hill.
- Stare back at a heron.
- Marvel at the mating ritual of two birds.
- Look at a mountain and think how long it would take one person to cart it away, or make one, or climb it.
- Think about how a human could make a tree.
- Consider a mother duck and her little chicks.

3. *Study.* Some people will most sense the presence of God as a result of study. This will primarily be the study of God's Word, but Christian literature can also minister to our lives.

Suggested Application: Set aside some "TAWG" about five days a week—between five and thirty minutes—to read your Bible. Ask your Christian bookstore for a good book on the character of God to supplement your Bible study.

4. *Music.* Some people are gifted with a good voice or at least can appreciate a good voice. These people will find that singing hymns and choruses of worship and praise will bring them quickly into the presence of Christ.

Suggested Application: Buy a hymnal or bring home music sheets handed out for sing-a-longs. Then in the quiet hours of dawn or late night, sing of his amazing grace, how great he is, and how great is his faithfulness.

5. *Prayer.* Prayer is the act of speaking and listening to God. Some people will find they most sense God when they are communicating with him in prayer.

Suggested Application: Spend some "structured" time every day pouring out your heart to God. Then, intentionally quiet yourself to discern impressions from the Holy Spirit (that agree with God's Word). Throughout the day pray about everything in silent prayers with your eyes open, as though in simple everyday conversation with a deeply respected friend and counselor.

6. *Service.* For some people the presence of God is most felt when serving him. In the faithful employment of their spiritual gifts they sense an inner joy that reminds them of God's presence. This may be either through their vocation, a ministry of the church, or both. It may be through acts of "building the kingdom" or "tending the culture."

Suggested Application: Ask your pastor for a service opportunity which makes use of your spiritual gifts. Concentrate on recalibrating your view of work to accommodate the truth of Colossians 3:23.

7. *Fellowship.* Some people are relationship oriented, and they most feel the presence of Christ through the bond of fellowship with brothers and sisters in the Lord. These people are the ones always first to arrive and last to leave Sunday school or a home Bible study.

Suggested Application: The next time you are with a group of believers, after the meeting (while munching on a second cookie), ask someone to tell you how he or she came to faith in Christ.

8. *Hearing the Word.* Some people will best sense God through the preaching of his Word. This is traditionally viewed as the predominant means of grace.

Suggested Application: Listen carefully for the biblical truth and principles in your pastor's sermons. Then consider how God himself is speaking to you through the pastor's words. Talk with your spouse or a friend about how you could apply the message to your life.

ACCOUNTABILITY

It has always been my practice to hold periodic staff meetings to review progress toward goals we've set and problems we're trying to solve. I do this because I know that even when we all leave a meeting headed in the same direction, things change over a period of days and weeks.

One person veers off too far to the right. Another to the left. Someone becomes confused and starts wandering around in circles. It's good to come back together, get refocused, and start out again.

It's the same in all of life. Even when we have the right starting point—Christ—we will veer off the path without regular accountability. One suggestion to keep on track is to meet periodically with a few other like-minded people. Our organization, Man in the Mirror, distributes a free wallet-sized accountability card that you can use to "check" yourself on all the major areas of life. (Call 407-331-0095 extension 15 if you are interested.)

The challenge is to stop trying to change God and to start being changed by God. It is to come humbly to the foot of the cross of Christ, kneel in repentance, and negotiate the terms of a full, total, complete surrender to the lordship of Jesus Christ. That is the chief task of finding authenticity at midlife.

FOCUS QUESTIONS

1. Are you in a "structural hurry" and if so, how?
2. How much like cardboard has your relationship with God been, and why or why not?
3. When is the last time you experienced the presence of God in what this chapter described as the "moment of humility"? How appealing is the idea of building a daily moment of humility into

your life? What adjustment would you need to make to spend more time with God?

4. Which of the eight practical ideas mentioned most appeal to you and why? Do you want to apply any of the suggestions? If so, what do you plan to do?

NINETEEN

Reinventing Your Marriage—New Compatibility and Mature Love

You and your mate are the only two people who are really in this thing together. All others will phase in and out of your life, even children . . . hopefully.

A COUPLE TOOK A LONG-ANTICIPATED TEN-DAY vacation to London. When they returned I asked the wife, "What was your favorite part of London?"

Without hesitation she said, "Walking down the street arm in arm, together—alone."

You and your spouse are the only two people who are really in this thing together. All others will phase in and out of your lives—even children . . . hopefully.

Hearing this, one man said, "When you see it like that, I guess it's pretty important to pick the right mate." It is important to pick a good mate, but it's even more important to work at the mate you picked. Even the perfect mate selection will end up as a bad relationship if we don't work at it.

THE PROBLEM

Recently I was having an argument with Patsy. Well into my pontificating speech I found myself shrieking, "Woman, when are you going to get that problem worked out? That's the same problem we were dealing with in the first month of our marriage!"

Later, after I calmed down and apologized, something dawned on me. Since then I have confirmed this principle by informal surveys among several hundred people. Think carefully about this next sentence:

The problems you struggle with during your first year of marriage are, by degrees, the same problems you will still be struggling with at the ten-, twenty-, and even thirty-year mark of your marriage.

Unless we take personal responsibility to become the spouse God intends, we can spend our entire lives repeating, by degrees, the same mistakes and sins we committed in our first year of marriage.

THE DIVORCE OPTION

In her book *New Passages*, author Gail Sheehy suggests that in our sexually revolutionized culture people will pick different marriage partners for different phases of their lives. We must categorically reject that idea. Divorce is not a viable option. "'I hate divorce,' says the LORD God" (Malachi 2:16).

Practically speaking, most divorced people wish they had worked harder at their marriages. A man told his secretary he was divorcing his wife. His secretary said, "You're not very smart. You think you're going to get rid of all your problems. You're not. You're weak. In two years you will be remarried and you will have another set of marriage problems just as bad if not worse than the first." By the time I met him he could append his secretary's comments with, "She was right."

Your commitment to the institution of marriage is more important than your commitment to your mate. I'm not saying your commitment to your mate isn't important—it's crucial. But unless we have an even greater moral commitment to the institution of marriage itself, then what is the glue that will hold us to our marriage vows when we go through the inevitable stages of simply not liking each other very much? With that thought in mind, in this chapter we will discuss ways to "work at the mate you picked" that will lead to a deeper love and intimacy.

EMOTIONALLY UNPLUGGED

As a Tom Clancy reader I was saddened to read that he and his wife, Wanda, had separated after twenty-eight years of marriage. At the time, the ages of their four children were eleven to twenty-three. To summarize, for this to happen, a lot of people will have to go through a lot of pain.

There is ultimately one major reason couples don't make it. One or both partners become "emotionally unplugged" from the other, and they don't work together to get replugged.

What can we do about that? To be emotionally plugged in to each other requires that we love our mates the way they want to be loved.

FINDING THE RIGHT LOVE LANGUAGE

Patsy and I had the serendipity of learning about Gary Chapman's book, *The Five Love Languages*.

For the first twenty-three years of our marriage I loved Patsy the way I wanted to be loved. I feel loved when Patsy spends large blocks of quality time with me. Since that's the way I want to be loved, I assumed that was the way to best love her. So I smothered Patsy with long talks and doing things together.

For twenty-three years Patsy loved me the way she wanted to be loved. She feels loved when I help out with household chores, run errands, or do small acts of kindness. Since that's the way she wants to be loved, she assumed that was the way to best love me. For example, if I needed a clean shirt I might say, "That's okay, I'll just re-press this dirty one. Nobody will know the difference." She would always say, "No, that's okay. Really. I'd love to run to the cleaners for you."

Do yourself a favor and purchase Chapman's book. In case you don't, here's a general idea about the five different love languages:

- Words of affirmation: Compliments, kind words, notes, cards
- Quality time: One-to-one time, no interruptions, long walks, doing things together
- Receiving gifts: Fact-oriented information, gifts on special and not-so-special occasions
- Acts of service: "I can"; "I will"; "What else can I do?"; chores; repairs; kindnesses
- Physical touch: Nonverbals, verbals with word pictures, hugs, pats, kisses[1]

Aim to understand your own love language and the love language of your wife. Love your mate the way she wants to be loved, not the way you want to be loved. Also, help her understand how you need to be loved as well. In the second half, nothing will be more appreciated by your wife than loving her the way she wants to be loved.

CONVERSATION

My brother used to call me on the phone about once a week and tell me about the terrible things happening in his life. I remember that after his call one week I hung up feeling depressed and worried for him.

A few days later we all gathered at our parents' home on Sunday afternoon. There was my brother beaming with happiness, making himself the life of the party. "What are you so happy about?" I grumbled.

After this scenario repeated several times I finally figured out what was happening. Like many of us, ninety percent of my brother's life was positive, but ten percent was negative. When he would call me, however, one hundred percent of our conversation revolved around the negative ten percent. So, one hundred percent of my understanding of how he was doing was based on the negative ten percent he was telling me. I didn't know the other ninety percent even existed.

How can that happen? The tendency for most of us is to speak about what's broken and not working right. We speak out of our pain. We speak about the dissonance in our lives.

It can be the same way in our marriages. A lovely couple could not resolve their conflicts because their arguments always became so emotional. Because they tended to speak out of their feelings, their exchanges were filled with superlatives and generalizations. Their verbal barbs were out of proportion and lacked a sense of perspective for how the total relationship was going.

Both husband and wife were quick to express these exaggerated "feelings" when they were upset with each other. They did not, however, balance those words out by also speaking positive encouragements and affirmations when they were content. In other words, almost one hundred percent of their verbal communication was about the ten percent or so that wasn't going well. The end result was that virtually all of their verbal communication revolved around conflict. The positive remained cloistered away in nonverbal thoughts. Verbally, they shared very little about the positive and deeper aspects of life.

Our "outside" verbal communication needs to accurately reflect the quality of what's happening "inside" our relationship. This means we must speak rationally, not just emotionally. Our conversation with each other needs to reflect the fullness of how it's going—plus point to where we want the relationship to go.

The best way to insure that what's said "outside" reflects what's happening "inside" is to set aside daily time for conversation. Our research showed that conversation is the number one desire wives have of their husbands. My wife and I have discovered for ourselves that when we don't have meaningful daily conversation, affirming and encouraging words are left unsaid. (Whether we meet or not, however, I still always seem to find a way to work in my criticisms.)

Every precious moment a couple shares together is like another inch of growth to the root system of their marriage. The deep roots of an old oak tree make it hard to knock down.

You and your mate will obviously not agree on everything. You don't need to. What you do need from each other, however, is to feel understood. In other words, when Patsy thinks differently on a subject than I do, I nevertheless want to feel like she understands where I'm coming from. I want to be able to say, "Yes! That's my position. We may not agree, but at least I feel you accurately understand where I'm coming from." Only when your spouse believes you understand her position can she listen—really listen—with an open mind.

In thinking over how to optimize the second half of marriage, nothing seems more valuable than regular, accurate communication. Accuracy means giving a proportionate amount of verbal expression to the ninety percent positive as well as the ten percent negative. Accuracy in the second half means to go ahead and say the positive things we may have left unsaid in the first half. It also means learning to leave unsaid what, in the past, we said too quickly.

THREATS TO UNCONDITIONAL LOVE

I would like to mention a huge issue for the second half. Many spouses take any question about their behavior—weight, appearance, providing, spending habits, cooking, use of free time, housekeeping—

as a threat to unconditional love. There has to be a basis to discuss issues without it being taken as a threat to unconditional love.

To talk about sensitive subjects with our mates we must have "a sense of occasion." There are right and wrong times to bring up such issues. When you have a legitimate concern or issue to discuss with your spouse, "elevate the moment." Create a sense that what you have to say is beyond the norm. Give it special significance.

For example, let's say you are unhappy about how household chores are shared. Rather than simply saying so, elevate the moment by saying, "Honey, when it's convenient I would like to sit down with you at the dining room table and spend thirty minutes discussing some thoughts I have about household chores." This has the salutary effect of preparing your partner for an "important" conversation.

When you actually have your "elevated" conversation, keep the focus on yourself. Talk about how you feel on the subject, not about your mate. For example, don't say, "You don't care about me because you don't pay attention to the way you dress." Notice this sentence goes at "you" twice. Talking about your mate instead of the issue itself will be taken as an attack on her identity as a person. Better to say, "Honey, when you don't pay attention to the way you dress I feel like I'm not that important to you." This helps to keep the conversation focused on how you feel, not the other person. It also keeps the blood pressure down.

Still, though, we must not make our mates feel that our love actually is conditional. A couple was struggling in their marriage. The husband asked his sister for counsel. She replied, "Cal, you are a demanding person." When your wife feels she must meet certain standards before your love is released, she cannot relax around you.

Suppose a husband with perfectionistic tendencies constantly critiques his mate. Though he may love his spouse unconditionally, his wife feels she must perform to be approved. Who's at fault? What should they do?

God accepts us as we are. He does not critique our non-sinful behavior. We do not have to perform for God's approval. His love for us is unconditional. He is our model for loving our spouse.

THE LOSS OF YOUTH

One day during midlife you will look at your spouse and think, "There's been a mistake! I can't be married to a person that old!" On the day one man hit this stage he said, "When I hugged my wife today I felt like I was hugging my mother. This can't be happening."

You may resent that your mate is getting older, especially if you think you are not. I've got news for you. You are too. One of the biggest problems in reaching the middle years is the perception that your mate got older, while you haven't changed that much. Why is that?

In the early stages of midlife you have been astonished to learn someone who looks considerably older (at least in your own mind) is your same age. When you don't feel any older at forty or fifty than you did at thirty, it's hard to imagine much has changed. It has.

During midlife gravity takes over. Things sag. At a recent wedding one mother commented to another, "If we wore those bridesmaid dresses no one would be able to tell the front from the back!"

Tics become permanent. Hair falls out. Memory fades. Absent-mindedness becomes daily, even routine. Remember all those things your parents said that you swore you would never say when you got to be their age? We say them all, don't we?

When these things overtake you and your wife, what should you do? The answer is to reinvent your ideal of marriage for the second half. This takes time, perhaps a couple of years. The key item is to relax and be patient. Unfortunately, when I went through this phase I started putting a lot of pressure on my wife to "recover" her youth. Can't be done.

After going that direction for a year, I slowly began to accept her for who she had become, as God had accepted me for who I had become. Yet, we will go through periods when little black clouds of negative thoughts, anger, and withdrawal put us in conflict.

This too shall pass. We must give ourselves time to catch up emotionally to what we know to be true intellectually. Objectively, a man said, "I have a great wife and a great life." Subjectively, however, it took him over two years to "process" his changing feelings. It is good to remember the ultimate objective of our marriages: To grow old with a friend, satisfied with the past.

If you and your mate have two different visions of what your marriage will be in the future, one of you will have to go through the death of your vision. Of necessity, the vision that must die is the one that is trying to hold on to youth, a vision of the past, or a long-held desire that's never going to happen. If your spouse has not been a "talker" for twenty-five years, chances are she will not be a talker for the next twenty-five years. You have to accept it. You have to let go of the expectation. You have to renew your vision around the positives that are there, not the negatives you wish were not.

It is difficult to "give out" at a level of relationship and intimacy that is not returned in kind. To find peace you may have to accept that your mate will never be as "romantic" as you are. Could it be that God has called you to fill in that gap in your mate? And for your mate to fill in the gaps you have?

Most importantly, this transition takes time. Many divorces take place at this passage because one partner wasn't willing to be patient for feelings to adjust to the new reality. Others are simply too selfish to accept their mates. One man was sure the grass was greener on the other side of the fence. When he got there and looked down, he saw huge bare spots all over. It all depends on the angle from which you're looking.

It's important not to dwell on negative feelings. Instead, put them into proportion considering the whole marriage. If you and your mate are Christian people, then you have to do what Christian people do.

FEELING SUPPORT

One of the deeply felt needs of the midlife marriage is to feel wanted, needed, and appreciated. These needs surge to flood stage. Your mate is wrestling to find peace and accept new limitations. She may not have the old self-confidence for a time.

It is a wise spouse who will be sensitive to a mate's vulnerability at midlife. Take the initiative to build up your mate's self-esteem. Help her remember that our identity is in Christ, not our circumstances. Encourage her to believe that the best days of life are still ahead.

Ironically, you may need to put in special effort to reach out to your mate at the very time she is withdrawing from you. This will take the special courage that comes from unconditional love and commitment.

RECONNECTING THROUGH NURTURING

I would like to suggest that a woman's inner beauty cannot fully bloom and flourish unless her husband nurtures her inner being.

Bill McCartney, founder of Promise Keepers and former head coach of the University of Colorado national champion football team, once heard a visiting preacher say, "You can tell the depth of a man's walk with God by looking at the countenance of his wife's face."

McCartney says he turned and looked at that moment into his wife's eyes and realized that he had neglected the nurture of his beloved wife. He resigned his position as the head coach at Colorado. Most people assumed it was to devote more time to Promise Keepers. Actually, he wanted to reconnect with his wife.

Husbands, by and large, do not have a vision for nurturing their wives. One of our greatest failings as husbands has been our failure to nurture our wives. Men, we must confess that we have focused on the outward appearance without investing ourselves to nurture "the unfading beauty of a gentle and quiet spirit" (1 Peter 3:4).

THE BLESSING OF TOUCHING EACH OTHER

Recently a man in his late sixties said, "The other day I was talking to Clara, and I reached over and squeezed her forearm while I spoke—just a little. You know, she turned into a little kitten right before my eyes! I had no idea how much it meant to her!"

I learned about the power of touch twenty years ago in a seminar taught by author and speaker Russ Campbell. Since then, whenever I walk by Patsy when she's reading or sitting down, I will reach over and softly place my hand on top of her head, then move on without a word. I believe this has been a gift of love to my wife.

Women especially find touch so important. Encourage your wife with more "touch." Nonsexual touching includes quick hugs, long embraces, pats on the arms or shoulders, squeezes of the knee or hand, putting your arm around the shoulder, walking through the mall holding hands, kisses, and sitting on the sofa close enough to touch when you watch TV.

PHYSICAL INTIMACY

I don't know any other way to say it: Sex in the second half is better! During the first half sex often tended to be a physical act. Without emotional intimacy, physical intimacy is merely a biological function.

By the second half two things have happened. First, you have history. You have been through "things" together, hard things. These tests have made your marriage stronger. The more you have risked with someone, the stronger the emotional bond. By midpoint the bond becomes forever soldered together.

Second, you have surprising amounts of sexual energy and appetite. The kids are gone and you have time to focus on each other. You have mellowed, and you are more into serving your spouse than ever before. It's a great life.

TIME ALONE

Patsy and I have discovered a new type of date. We both love to read. We go to lunch at Barnes and Noble or Borders, then each get to purchase one book or magazine.

During the second half one of the largest adjustments is reordering the new time that's available when the nest empties. Be intentional. Yes, it's certainly time to pursue the hobby you shelved in your twenties or pick up a new one. If possible, take up hobbies you can do together. On the other hand, having a hobby of your own will allow you some space, not to mention give a block of free time to your mate.

What are some things you could do together? Here are a few suggestions:

- Buy a two-seat sailboat.
- Get season tickets to the theater or a sports team.
- Start hiking the trails in your area.
- Visit a hobby store for ideas.

- Without regard to cost, make a list of the five things you have most wanted to do.
- Plan a special vacation together at least six months away.
- Buy a bed and breakfast directory and take special nights occasionally.
- Take up gardening together.
- Take walks together.
- Go bowling.
- Get a dog.
- Start a home business.
- Volunteer at a local ministry.
- Teach a young married Sunday school class.

SATISFACTION WITH MARRIAGE

Be encouraged. Marriage has its ups and downs, but a recent study reveals that your happiest days together are ahead of you.

With this piece of positive news, make sure you do the "time" necessary to fill your second half with the second wind of joyful companionship. As you consider your marriage, which subjects in this chapter will most determine the success and authenticity of your marriage in the

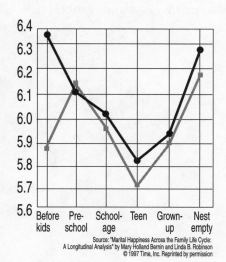

What do (Married) Men Want? Marriage has its ups and downs (the low point for both sexes is when kids are teens), but a new study pinpoints a further discrepancy between male and female happiness: husbands are notably more satisfied than wives when there are no children.

Source: "Marital Happiness Across the Family Life Cycle:
A Longitudinal Analysis" by Mary Holland Bernin and Linda B. Robinson
© 1997 Time, Inc. Reprinted by permission

second half? In the next and final chapter we will look at your career options.

Focus Questions

1. If you're married, have you had enough time together as a couple? Why or why not?

2. "It is important to pick a good mate, but it's even more important to work at the mate you picked." Do you agree or disagree? Explain your answer.

3. To what degree are you still struggling with the same problems you struggled with in your first year of marriage? What would it take for you to get by it?

4. "Your commitment to the institution of marriage is more important than your commitment to your mate." Do you agree or disagree? Explain your answer.

5. Do you have time set aside to have conversation with your spouse every or almost every day? If so, what has been the benefit? If not, what could it do for your marriage?

6. Your mate is getting older. Youth has yielded to maturity. Have you accepted this about your mate, or are you still trying to hold on to a vision that's never going to happen?

7. Does your spouse need to feel more of your support right now? What can you do about that?

TWENTY

Midlife Career Changes—Or Renewing the Career You Already Have

In vain you rise early and stay up late, toiling for food to eat—for he grants sleep to those he loves.

PSALM 127:2

*B*Y THE AGE OF THIRTY-SIX STEPHEN had achieved more than he ever dreamed possible. That was the year he became a full partner in a major New York investment banking firm, responsible for many of their largest accounts—a who's who of some of America's most important corporations. By the age of forty-two he had more money than he could have imagined.

The cost was steep. He said, "What really became valuable to me was not money but time. The few arguments I've had with my wife have been mostly about time. My job is ruthless like that. That's just what the clients expect. Whatever it takes. If that means staying up all night to hit a deadline, then that's what you do. If it means not leaving the office until nine o'clock every night, then that's what you do."

He found himself kissing his three young kids good night on Sunday evening and, the next thing he knew, they were waking him up on Saturday morning. At one time he had been an elder in his church, but when they asked him to serve another term he had to pass. His priorities were God, family, then business. He really believed his family was his primary mission field. But that's not what was happening. He said, "In my company, spouses are almost nonexistent."

One day he was reading an article in the *Wall Street Journal*. The founder of a major exchange-listed technology company abruptly left his CEO position to become a part-time employee back in the lab.

One year earlier that man and his wife had sat down and asked each other, "What are our priorities?" He told his wife he thought their priorities were "God, family, sports, and business—in that order." When they looked at their list, they realized how they spent their time was inversely proportioned to their priorities. They decided to post their priorities on the refrigerator, and then they spent a year looking at their list and thinking it over. At the end of that year is when they made their move.

Stephen said, "That really hit me. Those were pretty much my priorities—God, family, then work. But that's not what I was saying with how I spent my time." That's when he started searching. He read a lot. He prayed. He asked for prayer. He began networking with businessmen. He explored joining a ministry.

Stephen's theology understood that both ministry and business are equally valid. "So the question on my mind was, 'Where can I serve God better?'" Ultimately, it really had to boil down to calling and gifts.

"We prayed a lot," he said. "It was an agonizing one-year struggle. I didn't know what I was going to do. I just knew I had to make a change. That was tough because I had always known where I was going, what I was going to do. Yet, it was a season of wonderful growth. I became more dependent on God, and I don't want to lose that."

Meanwhile, he told his bosses that he couldn't keep going at the same pace. They were very sympathetic and eventually offered him a position as chairman of one of their subsidiaries. That meant moving to another city, but they decided not to buy a new house there until their existing house sold. Their house sat on the market for seven months! Real estate brokers kept saying to them, "We can't believe your house hasn't sold yet."

Still, Stephen yearned to find a new life, to become part of an organization whose values more resembled his own. For several months he had been talking to a company owner who was looking for someone with his skills. He was eventually offered a position.

"After much prayer we took the offer and couldn't be happier. Frankly, though, I thought my new calling would include deprivation. I was suspicious of the offer because it was exciting, and provided the opportunity to make some good money, the work would be rewarding, we would get to live in a great city, and our kids would go to a terrific school. And would you believe it—our house sold three days after we accepted the position."

Most of us will not experience such a near-perfect transition into new careers, if we change at all. Yet, because God is good, our lives will not turn out like we plan, but better.

The Problem

A vigorous fifty-two-year-old CEO of a company with thousands of employees resigned at the zenith of his career. When I asked him why he said, "I would rather leave five years too early than five minutes too late."

He added, "I'm not concerned about my career position for the next ten years. It's the one after that which concerns me. That's the one I really need to plan for now as I consider my next position." Good point.

Some of us are blessed with such boldness at the midpoint. These are men fortunate enough to "show well" in their forties and fifties. To them, the issue is not whether they will find a challenge that fits for the second half but rather what that challenge will be.

Most, however, have not experienced success at the highest levels of the corporate executive suite. They're not in "high demand" at the midpoint of their productive lives. They find themselves a bit more tentative as they ponder their careers for the second half. However, they have nevertheless enjoyed a meaningful career. For the second half they want to increase, not decrease their sense of contribution.

At their midpoint many midlifers find themselves stuck in vocations for which they are ill-suited by aptitude or interest. They have stagnated. They do not sense they are making a difference.

At midlife the window of opportunity for meaningful contribution becomes visibly finite, and a sense of panic can set in. When we look at a ten-, twenty-, or twenty-five-year horizon we wonder, *Because I lived, how will the world be a better place?*

Many despair of making a significant impact on the world. They settle for making a living instead of a contribution. In this chapter let's think through what will give you a second wind vocationally for the second half.

Rest assured. It may take some time to sort things out, even a few years. By God's grace, though, you will find a vocation in which you can make a meaningful contribution, find significance, and help leave the world a better place. Really.

A HIGHER VERSUS A DIFFERENT CALLING

A man said, "At forty-three I know I am not going to be the millionaire I thought I'd be at twenty-three, but I would like to do something significant. The years keep going by faster. I am a good salesman, husband, and father, and I want to be remembered for that—but not only that. I want to leave a legacy. There must be a higher calling than to be a salesman all my life."

This is perhaps the most frequently heard comment about work at the midpoint. The correct answer is, no, there is no "higher" calling, but there may well be a "different" calling. There are four possibilities for a "different" calling for men led to reinvent their careers.

Option #1: Rebuild Your View of Vocation

First, you may need only to rebuild your view of vocation. A man began teaching high school math after college. He said, "After a few years I have identified two problems I think God is calling me to deal with.

"First, my students are coming to class with problems that math can't solve. Second, the Christian teachers at my school don't know each other." He is praying for a vision about how to respond to these two needs. He says, "I am an ordained math teacher."

Often we denigrate our jobs, thinking they're of little consequence to the larger work of God. Oh, we may not speak publicly this way, but in our heart of hearts we can't see how our work makes any difference.

Nothing could be further from the truth. Your work does matter to God. Most of us will spend eighty to ninety-five percent of our vocational time devoted to God's calling to "tend the culture" and only the balance of five to twenty percent helping to "build the kingdom."

There is intrinsic value in our work because it makes life more livable, creates jobs, contributes to an orderly society, creates income to meet family obligations, satisfies our need to be significant, and fulfills the biblical mandate to "fill, rule, and subdue" God's creation.

The first time my new FedEx man stepped out of his van to deliver my package I suspected two things: first, that he loved God; second, that he understood that his job has intrinsic value. His manner, earnest yet content, accompanied by a quick smile, spoke volumes. It's not just that our work is something we do to give us a platform to serve God, it *is* serving God.

If you have a Bible concordance, look up all the references to "secular." How many did you find? None, right? That's because God makes no distinction between "sacred" and "secular." The notion that we perform secular jobs or go into the ministry is a cultural idea, not a biblical one.

Every vocation is holy to the Lord. Our vocation, or work, is an extension of our personal relationship with God. Most of us will never be in "occupational" ministry, but that doesn't mean we are not ministers. The Bible teaches that all Christians are ministers. So, the issue isn't whether or not you are in ministry, but whether or not you are faithful in the ministry God has given you.

If you are a waiter, every customer that sits in your station is a divine appointment—an opportunity for you to be the incarnation of the loving character of Jesus Christ. If you are a salesman, every appointment is holy and (God knows) every sale is sacred. If you are a manager, every conflict between two employees is an opportunity for you to demonstrate the reconciling nature of our Lord.

Option #2: Change Jobs or Vocations

Second, for reasons already discussed you may be a candidate for a change. Perhaps you are underemployed, underpaid, underchallenged, or underappreciated. When Phil Jackson, head coach of the NBA champion Chicago Bulls, was approached by the Orlando Magic, he made it clear his issues were not control or money, but feeling wanted and appreciated. If you can't work it out, by all means change.

People tend to be innovators, adapters, or adopters. Which of these three categories best fits you? If you are an innovator and you have a job that requires you to adopt an existing system "as is" you are in the wrong slot. If you are an adapter you need an association with an innovator who is willing to let others shape and refine his or her ideas. It is pure torture to be an adopter—say a salesman—who is asked to innovate by writing a sales and marketing policy manual. If you are in the wrong slot, discuss this with your employer. Find out what both of you consider your strengths. Ask to be placed in a position that optimizes what you can contribute. If your employer won't work with you, you may want to make a change.

You may be bored and need a new challenge. You may realize you will never find "substance" as you have come to view it in your present position. If you don't like what you do, by all means make a change. A lawyer who had "done it all" bought a half interest in a potting soils wholesale company. Changing spouses may be a no-no, but changing your job may be exactly what's needed to reenergize you and give you new purpose. A fifty-five-year-old accountant, unhappy in his work, was asked, "If you could do anything in the world you wanted, what would it be?" He answered, "I would really like to be a mail man." Why not? Unfortunately for him, he never made the switch.

A friend was a minority partner in a contracting business. The senior partner, a workaholic, constantly pressured him to work seventy-hour weeks, including Sundays. My friend wanted to lead a balanced life. Even though it meant a reduction of income, he found a position that allowed him to work a forty-five-hour week. He says, "It saved my marriage and gave me back my private life. The stress level dropped immediately." You may want to make a change to get your priorities in balance.

One problem in later midlife is marketability. A man in his early fifties said, "I was caught in a downsizing. I found out quickly that the premium is on younger people. It was quite a blow to my self-esteem to have all this skill overlooked in favor of someone half my age." A change should be carefully planned. Don't jump too quickly just to get out of a difficult work situation. Change *to* something, not *from* something.

Option #3: Take Up "Tentmaking" Ministry

A forty-two-year-old man who has built a solid business over the last fifteen years said, "I'm set. Financially I'm doing well. I've got all my systems in place. I'm looking around. I'd like to do something significant." By "significant" he was referring to an activity that would "mean something" in the larger sense of an eternal perspective.

If you want to have a larger impact you may be a candidate for a "tentmaking" ministry. A "tentmaker" is someone who maintains both a career and a ministry. The term was coined after the apostle Paul who became a missionary but continued his vocation of tentmaking to pay his way.

The concept is most often applied to foreign missionaries who could not get into a country unless as a consultant, physician, accountant, or other occupation. It is also a useful idea for today's unhappy or restless midlifer.

The advantages are numerous. For some, remaining in the work force provides a better platform for ministering to people also in the work force. It may give you access to needy people unreachable by any others. By acting as a self-funding "tentmaker" you are not a financial burden to others. And no one can charge you with "doing it for the money."

A number of categories to help you think about a tentmaking ministry approach follow:

Bivocational. It wasn't until I was forty that I realized I had always been "bivocational." In the early years I was ninety percent real estate and ten percent ministry. Then it was seventy-five–twenty-five. Then fifty–fifty. Then twenty-five–seventy-five. In my case, I led Bible studies, chaired the annual Thanksgiving Leadership Prayer Breakfast, helped local ministries, served on a ministry board, and regularly met with men one-on-one.

If you own your own company or control your own time you may want to consider describing yourself by the category "bivocational." Perhaps you could start an outreach to troubled inner-city kids. Maybe you can use your influence to reach your peers for God.

Professional Tithe. If you spend fifty hours a week practicing law or mowing lawns, why not consider giving a "tithe" of your time to serving God. For example, if you are a computer programmer working forty hours per week, you could "tithe" four hours a week to help a local ministry with their programming problems.

A two-year-old boy from a family of limited means needed heart surgery. The mother told the doctor, "We can't have the surgery because we can't afford it." The doctor responded, "My father was also a doctor and he told me that a certain percentage of my patients wouldn't be able to afford to pay, so that's okay. I will still do the surgery."

Elder or Deacon. If you have gifts in "shepherding" people, leadership, administration, or teaching you may want to candidate for church leadership. These positions require a few hours a week, but they will take all the time you feel led to give. Probably most of the elders the apostle Paul appointed over the early churches maintained their vocations.

Church or Ministry Volunteer. Many men hold posts in their churches like usher, Sunday school teacher, bus driver, and the like. If you hold a position of such responsibility that the system will break down if you don't show up, you can probably consider yourself a tentmaker. All churches and many ministries, however, need responsible, dependable part-time volunteers who will be faithful to do the "smaller" jobs.

Free Agent. Over the years the single largest group of tentmakers I have known I would term "free agents." These men and women are consumed with serving God in the daily routines of their lives. They view everything they do vocationally as serving the Lord. In addition to attacking their work as "unto the Lord" they also look for "spiritual opportunities" to help people in every encounter.

Such a man arranged for his employer to join him for a luncheon appointment with a potential major customer. As the waiter brought the food he asked the prospect, "Would you mind if I say a blessing for our food?" At this point his boss tried to slide under the table with embarrassment at the same time steam poured out his ears. The prospective customer brightened and said, "That would be great!"

Option #4: Pursue Vocational Ministry

Fourth, you may answer a call to vocational ministry. Increasingly, men and women in their middle years are hearing and answering a call into occupational ministry.

For many, this appears to be an attractive and logical direction. They burn with a desire to make a contribution, and occupational ministry seems a natural outlet.

A word of caution, however. It is generally said to people sensing a call to ministry, "If you can do anything else and be happy, then don't pursue the ministry." This is not because the calling is so high or so difficult, but because so many have made mistakes when the call they "heard" was little more than a strong self-will. Some move too quickly "on the rebound" from a crisis experience.

If you sense that God may be calling you to occupational ministry, authenticate your calling. You belong to a spiritual community. This community has a long history you can tap into. They have experience in helping people authenticate their calls. If you don't get support from the people who know you, this should be a huge red flag.

Check with your pastor, the elders or deacons of your church, your spouse, your children. Do you have any track record in ministry that suggests you would be successful? Are you already doing in part what you want to do full time? Do you have a burning desire for ministry? If so, has your desire led to current action or have you just been talking about it?

In my own case, I changed callings from real estate developer to ministry, but it came slowly. I began sensing a call "toward" ministry over two years before I sensed a call "to" ministry. It took another three and a half years after that before a vision of exactly what I was to do took shape. In the meantime, I began taking seminary courses, continued a very active ministry to men in our community, and spent time authenticating my call with my pastor and Christian leaders with whom I had relationships. The time span from first inkling to selling my main business was nearly six years.

CONCLUSION

In the end everything boils down to calling. This issue is, "What is God's call on your life?" This often doesn't come easily. And when it does come, it is usually followed by a season of equipping in which God works things into and out of our lives. Then, when we have been fully equipped and prepared for the battle, he sends. God has a special purpose for the second half of your life. Seek and you will find.

FOCUS QUESTIONS

1. Have you enjoyed a meaningful career so far? Why or why not?
2. What have you had to sacrifice to get where you are vocationally? Has it been worth the price?
3. How much in demand do you think you are right now? How tentative are you about your future vocational prospects? Have you experienced any sense of panic and, if so, why?
4. We all want to make an impact and leave the world a better place. Often, though, we underestimate the potential of our present position. Often we are not proactive enough to reshape the career we already have. Often we think the grass is greener. Do you think you can find a second wind for the second half in your present position? How about in your present career field? Whichever way you answer, what should you do now?
5. Which of the four options discussed in this chapter seem attractive to you, and why? What's your next step?

AFTERWORD

YOU PROBABLY PICKED UP THIS BOOK because you found yourself or someone you love in a midlife slump. I hope you have found it helpful. It would surprise me, however, if you came out the other side of the midlife lake during this reading, at least completely.

I hope, though, that you've seen your life from a fresh angle, thought some new thoughts, remembered some old truths, and made peace with some of the changes taking place.

The simple cure for a midlife funk is the passage of time. The difficult part is to not make any decisions now you will regret later when you feel differently. Take your time—especially in relationships.

As you return now to that unique set of relationships, tasks, problems, and opportunities that represents your second half, I pray God will fill your sails with a second wind. May you revel in the authenticity for which you long. It will come. Remember: Because God is good, your life will not turn out like you planned—it will turn out better.

ACKNOWLEDGMENTS

CREDIT FOR A WORK OF THIS magnitude belongs to a much broader group than a mere author.

First, to the hundreds of men whose lives have shaped these pages, thank you.

Many of the staff at Man in the Mirror saw less of me and covered for me as I was writing. Therefore, I feel a special debt of gratitude to those there who sacrificed, especially to David Delk, Gary Wyatt, John Horton, and Betty Feiler.

As always, my wife, Patsy, was my chief encourager and reader. Thank you.

The publishing team deserves the most gratitude. I simply could not have pulled the pieces together without the guidance, encouragement, and commitment of Robert Wolgemuth, John Sloan, and Mary McNeil.

PATRICK MORLEY

SINCE THE LATE 80's, Patrick Morley has been one of America's most respected authorities on the unique challenges and opportunities that men face. After spending the first part of his career in the highly competitive world of commercial real estate, Patrick has been used throughout the world to help men think more deeply about their lives.

In 1973 Patrick founded Morley Properties, which, for several years, was hailed as one of Florida's 100 largest privately held companies. During this time he was the president or managing partner of fifty-nine companies and partnerships. In 1989 he wrote *The Man in the Mirror*, a landmark book that poured from his own search for meaning, purpose, and a deeper relationship with God. This best-selling book captured the imaginations of hundreds of thousands of men worldwide. As a result, in 1991, Patrick Morley sold his business and founded Man in the Mirror, a ministry to men. Through his speaking and writing, he has become a tireless advocate for men, encouraging and inspiring them to change their lives in Christ. He has authored eight books.

"Our ministry exists," says Patrick Morley, "in answer to the prayers of all those wives, mothers, and grandmothers who have for decades been praying for the men in their lives."

Man in the Mirror's faculty members conduct church sponsored men's events nationwide. Patrick's dream is to network with other ministries and churches of all denominations to reach every man in America with a credible offer of salvation and the resources to grow in Christ.

Patrick Morley graduated with honors from the University of Central Florida, which selected him to receive its Distinguished Alumnus Award in 1984. He has completed studies at the Harvard Business School and Reformed Theological Seminary. Every Friday morning Patrick teaches a Bible study to 150 businessmen in Orlando, Florida, where he lives with his wife, Patsy, and dog, Katie. They have two grown children.

His website can be found at: *www.maninthemirror.com*

NOTES

Chapter 1: The New Meaning of Midlife—Not a Monolithic Experience

1. Gail Sheehy, *New Passages* (New York: Ballantine, 1995), 4.
2. For a person born in 1994 the average life expectancy is seventy-six years. By 2000 it will rise to seventy-seven years.
3. Statistical Abstract of the United States 1997, U. S. Department of Commerce, Economics and Statistics Administration, Bureau of the Census, Table 119.
4. William Bridges, *Transitions* (Reading: Addison-Wesley, 1980), 111.
5. Bob Buford, *Half Time* (Grand Rapids: Zondervan, 1994).

Chapter 2: A Wounded Dream—A Life That's Not Turning Out Like You Planned

1. Ellen Goodman, "'It's a Wonderful Life'—Midlife, That Is," *Orlando Sentinel*, December 24, 1996.
2. Ibid.

Chapter 3: A Raging Boredom—The Toll of Forty Years

1. Walter Anderson, *The Confidence Course* (New York: Harper-Collins, 1997), 32.

Chapter 5: The Shrinking Nest—Coping with the Loss

1. According to the Statistical Abstract of the United States 1997, 117th edition, U.S. Department of Commerce Economics and Statistical Administration, Bureau of Census, Table 620, seventy-five of every one hundred women ages 45–54 are already working, but when they reach ages fifty-five to sixty-four, employment actually decreases to fifty of every one hundred women. Over sixty-five, only nine of every one hundred women work.
2. Dave and Claudia Arp, *The Second Half of Marriage* (Grand Rapids: Zondervan, 1996), 40.

Chapter 6: A Stumbling Career—Dealing with Getting or Not Getting What We Want

1. Michael Novak, *Business As a Calling* (New York: The Free Press, 1996), 29.
2. R. C. Sproul, *God's Will and the Christian* (Wheaton: Tyndale, 1984), 67.
3. Ibid.

Chapter 7: Reconnecting with God—The Right Starting Point

1. Quoted in David F. Wells, *God in the Wasteland* (Grand Rapids: Eerdmans, 1994), 88.
2. Ibid., 108.
3. The technical term for man-centered, horizontal living is *anthropocentric*; for God-centered, vertical living it's *theocentric*.
4. William Strauss and Neil Howe, *The Fourth Turning* (New York: Broadway Books, 1997), 2.
5. Quoted in Billy Graham, *Just As I Am* (New York: HarperCollins/Zondervan, 1997), 194.
6. Quoted in William C. Placher, *A History of Christian Theology* (Philadelphia: Westminster, 1983), 279.
7. Market Facts' Telenation for *U.S. News and World Report* as reported in *USA Today*, June 20–22, 1997.
8. Dietrich Bonhoeffer, *The Cost of Discipleship* (New York: Macmillan, 1937, 1963), 45–48.

Chapter 8: Habitual Thinking—Defeating This Ally of Mediocrity

1. Stephen Hawking, *A Brief History of Time* (New York: Bantam, 1988), 22.
2. Roger von Oech, *A Whack on the Side of the Head* (New York: Warner, 1990), 26.

Chapter 9: Overcoming Bitterness—Seeking Forgiveness and Forgiving

1. Hannah Whitall Smith, *The Christian's Secret of a Happy Life* (Old Tappan: Spire, 1942), 28.

Chapter 10: Managing Expectations—The Key to Overcoming Disappointment

1. Kenneth Price, *The Eagle Christian* (Wetumpka, Alabama: Old Faithful, 1984), 21–25.

2. John 15:2.

Chapter 11: A Brush with Tragedy—When the Nature of Life Is Tragic

1. *Field of Dreams*, MCA Home Video, Inc., 1989.
2. Romans 8:28.

Chapter 12: Leftover Pain—How God Uses Sorrows That Won't Go Away

1. Philip E. Hughes, *The Second Epistle to the Corinthians* (Grand Rapids: Eerdmans, 1962), 442ff.

Chapter 13: Second Half Success—Recalibrating How You Measure Accomplishment

1. Joni Eareckson Tada, *The Greatest Lesson I've Ever Learned*, Vonette Bright, ed. (San Bernardino: Here's Life, 1990), 171–73.
2. Robert Bellah, et. al., *Habits of the Heart* (New York: Harper and Row, 1985), 290.

Chapter 14: Authenticity—To Move from Playing a Role to Being Your True Self

1. "Film Career Leaves Bette Midler Cold," *Orlando Sentinel*, April 20, 1997.
2. John R. O'Neill, *The Paradox of Success* (New York: Tarcher, 1994).

Chapter 16: Setting Priorities—The Passport to a Balanced Second Half

1. This idea is adapted from Patrick M. Morley, *Walking with Christ in the Details of Life* (Grand Rapids: Zondervan, 1992), 118.
2. Statistical Abstract of the United States 1997, U.S. Department of Commerce, Economics and Statistics Administration, Bureau of the Census, No. 119.

Chapter 17: A Cause to Champion—Writing a Life Mission Statement

1. Patrick M. Morley, *The Man in the Mirror* (Grand Rapids: Zondervan, 1997), 59–60, 64.

2. Michael Novak, *Business as a Calling* (New York: The Free Press, 1996), 35.

3. Warren Bennis and Burt Nanus, *Leaders* (New York: Harper Perennial, 1985), 89.

Chapter 18: Walking with God—Cultivating a Hunger for the God Who Is

1. Kenneth A. Myers, *All God's Children and Blue Suede Shoes* (Wheaton: Crossway, 1989), xiv.

Chapter 19: Reinventing Your Marriage—New Compatibility and Mature Love

1. Gary Chapman, *The Five Love Languages* (Chicago: Northfield, 1995).

2. William C. Placher, *A History of Christian Theology* (Philadelphia: Westminster, 1983), 279.

GENERAL INDEX

Scripture Index

The Rest of Your Life

Patrick Morley

*Are you completely satisfied with
the way your life is turning out?
If not, maybe it's time to do something extreme.*

Do you hunger for personal, spiritual revival? A reawakening in your life? Do you desire to recover a craving for the things of God? That longing in your heart for "more" can be completely satisfied. The life-changing passion you hunger for is actually available to you. You really can walk with Christ.

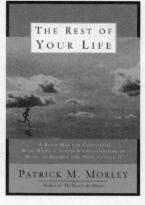

The Rest of Your Life will guide you from where you are now on your Christian journey to greater meaning and purpose, based on sound, biblical truth. It will move you to authentic Christianity in lifestyle and thinking.

The Rest of Your Life features four sections:

• Part 1, "Making Mid-Course Corrections," is a cultural analysis of the age, with focuses on the two spirits of our age, humanism, and a fifth gospel.

• Part 2, "Charting a New Course," helps you think your way from cultural to biblical Christianity.

• Part 3, "Deciding What to Believe," is the solid doctrinal teaching needed to move from relativistic thinking to biblical understanding.

• Part 4, "Cultivating an Authentic Christian Lifestyle," points the reader toward change, toward becoming a Great Commission Christian, toward actually doing God's will and completing the change to authentic Christian living.

Pick up your copy of *The Rest of Your Life* at local Christian bookstores and chart your course to finding authentic meaning and purpose!

Softcover 0-310-21767-9

Walking with Christ in the Details of Life

Patrick Morley

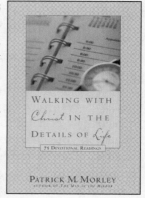

Putting Christ first in every dimension of life is one of the toughest challenges Christians face. Each day for a Christian is an opportunity for a vital, daily walk with the Lord. Yet there are so many things that are hard to understand and that pull a follower away from the daily path with Jesus. Total fulfillment for the Christian comes by walking with Christ in all these details of life.

Author Patrick Morley shows you how to gain maximum personal fulfillment by totally surrendering the details of your life to Christ. Morley reveals how to transform your life from partial to total obedience.

This book lays the groundwork for an intimate walk with Christ by confronting the temptations, the problems, and the doubts that keep Christians from this kind of surrender.

Here are some of the many practical questions you'll find answers to:

• I have such negative thoughts about so many people. How can I have victory over this problem?

• Sometimes I simply don't know how to pray. How should I pray when I can't find the words to express my hopes . . . my anguish?

• God isn't answering my prayers. How should I interpret His silence?

Walking with Christ in the Details of Life provides the insights and tools you need to enrich your life and experience a satisfying transformation to total surrender.

Softcover 0-310-21766-0

The Seven Seasons of a Man's Life

Patrick Morley

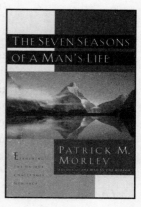

In his first book, author Patrick Morley looks at the basic problems men face and what the Bible says about them. Now, in *The Seven Seasons of a Man's Life*, Morley takes you more deeply into the seasons that affect a man's life, seasons that sometimes bring heartache and sometimes bring hope, but always bring the need to reexamine life in a biblical light.

You will find encouragement as you explore both hidden dangers and opportunities for personal growth in the seven seasons of your life:

- Reflection
- Building
- Crisis
- Renewal
- Rebuilding
- Suffering
- Success

Take a look at what others have to say about *The Seven Seasons of a Man's Life*:

"Patrick Morley challenges us to reflect honestly about ourselves—to see where we are in the context of life's seasons. I was tremendously moved. This should be required reading for every man!"

GARY SMALLEY—BEST-SELLING AUTHOR

"This is not just a good book, it's great. Patrick speaks to the issues, challenges your mind, and also penetrates your heart."

H. NORMAN WRIGHT—AUTHOR AND MARRIAGE COUNSELOR

"No one communicates with men at the level of Patrick Morley. The Seven Seasons of a Man's Life is another landmark work that will change thousands of lives, as did The Man in the Mirror."

STEPHEN ARTERBURN—COFOUNDER OF THE NEW LIFE CLINICS

Softcover 0-310-21764-4

The Man in the Mirror

Patrick Morley

"Uncommon wisdom ... stirring, disturbing, and abundantly encouraging...."

—Dr. R. C. Sproul

This book has established itself as a corner-stone in men's literature since its 1989 release. Winner of the prestigious Gold Medallion Award and appearing on the best-seller list eighteen times, it has helped thousands of men understand the person who stares back at them from the glass each morning and know what to do about their twenty-four most difficult problems.

The Man in the Mirror invites men to take a probing look at their identities, relationships, finances, time, temperament, and most important, the means to bring about lasting change.

If life's demands are constantly pressuring you to run faster and jump higher, this book is for you. Rich in anecdotes, thought-provoking questions, biblical insights, and featuring focus questions in each chapter suitable for personal or group use, this book offers a penetrating, pragmatic, and life-changing look at how to trade the rat race for the rewards of godly manhood.

Softcover 0-310-21768-7

ZondervanPublishingHouse
Grand Rapids, Michigan

A Division of HarperCollinsPublishers

We want to hear from you. Please send your comments about this book to us in care of the address below. Thank you.

ZondervanPublishingHouse
Grand Rapids, Michigan 49530
http://www.zondervan.com